An English Heritage I

Castle Rising

NORFOLK

R ALLEN BROWN MA, DLitt, FSA

Professor of History, University of London, King's College

English Heritage
London

Contents

Published by HMSO 1978, reprinted 1984
First published by English Heritage
(the Historic Buildings and Monuments Commission of England) 1987
and printed in England for HMSO

Dd 8975237 C50 9/87 47317
ISBN 1 85074 159 X

Illustrations

History

Castle Rising lies some 5 miles (8km) northeast of King's Lynn, near the Norfolk coast of the Wash. Like many places in East Anglia the village was formerly more important than it is now. According to local tradition, indeed, it was once a port of consequence, subsequently robbed of access to the sea by the silting up of the River Babingley. An ancient jingle (which those born and bred in these parts will have no difficulty in making rhyme) goes so far as to proclaim that:

Rising was a sea-port town, when Lynn was but a marsh,
Now Lynn it is a sea-port town, and Rising fares the worse.

This, however, would seem to owe something to artistic licence, as may also the Buck view of the castle (Plate 1) showing tall ships in the background as late as 1738. The records relating to the castle and manor which have been studied in the preparation of this handbook make no reference to any port here, though the lords of Rising, at least from the late eleventh century, had a valuable share in the customs of Lynn, which their present successors, the Dukes of Cornwall, still enjoy.

Rising certainly achieved the status of a borough in the Middle Ages and retained it until the nineteenth century, with its own mayor, recorder, high-steward and burgesses, and a corporate seal depicting the castle, as well as a fair

Plate 1 Engraving of Castle Rising from the southeast by Samuel and Nathaniel Buck, 1738

and market. It became a parliamentary borough also, first returning members to Parliament in 1558 and continuing to do so until the Reform Act of 1832. By that date its declining importance had made of it a textbook example of a rotten borough, though its members in its decayed state had included no less a figure than Sir Robert Walpole from neighbouring Houghton Hall. Now, apart from being a pleasant place, its particular claims to distinction are the castle, the church of the same date (albeit harshly restored in many parts in the nineteenth century by Salvin and others) and the charming hospital founded by the last lords of Rising, the Howards, in the reign of James I.

The castle, with its prodigious, man-made earthworks of great banks and ditches covering an area of some 12 acres (5ha), and its elegant yet powerful keep at bay within, is and always was among the most important in East Anglia. The roll-call of its several lords (and ladies)—from the Albini Earls of Sussex to the Howard Dukes of Norfolk, via the house of Montalt, Isabella (Queen and guilty wife of Edward II), the Black Prince and Prince Hal—makes its recorded history no less distinguished. This, one feels, is *par excellence* a great medieval lordly fortified residence—that is, a castle—at once a monument to the Norman Conquest and to that Anglo-Norman feudal society, French rather than English, which the Norman Conquest and settlement established in this country. Yet also, like the best ancient monuments perhaps, Rising does not reveal all its secrets but keeps some to itself, and in consequence its history, though distinguished, remains in some particulars enigmatic.

It is impossible to begin any account of the castle without turning at once to the formidable earthworks which are so much its dominating feature. As can be seen from the plan (page 6) they comprise: first an oval inner enclosure with the deepest ditches and biggest banks, with an early Norman gatehouse, of the same date as the keep, standing on its perimeter to the east, and containing both the keep itself and a small ancient ruined church or chapel almost buried in its northern bank; second, there is a rectangular banked and ditched enclosure, in places almost as strong, on the east of the central enclosure; third, there is a lesser rectangular enclosure on the west. In the past, and until recently, it has been customary to attribute all or part of these earthworks to a remoter antiquity than that of the Norman castle which occupies them—to the British, to the Saxon, but especially to the Roman period—as there has also been a general consensus of opinion that they are not all of the same date, most, though not all, theories making the outer works antedate the inner, thought to be cut into a pre-existing and much earlier large rectangular enclosure. [See the Glossary for an explanation of technical terms.]

Excavations carried out recently have gone a long way towards answering these questions, though, as often happens, they have also raised other questions of their own. Thus it is now known that all the earthworks, inner and outer (except a ditch of unknown date or purpose discovered inside and beneath the

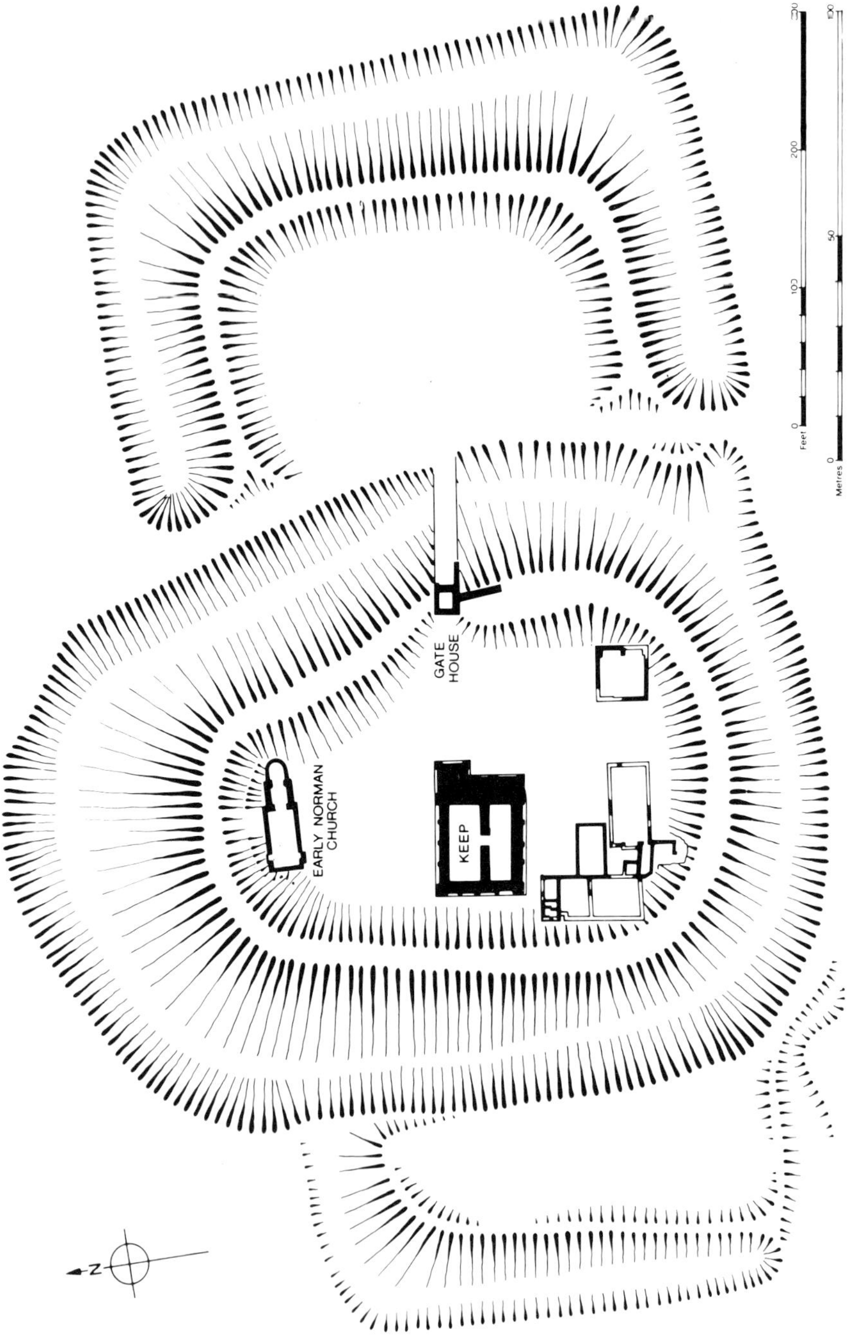

Plan of the castle

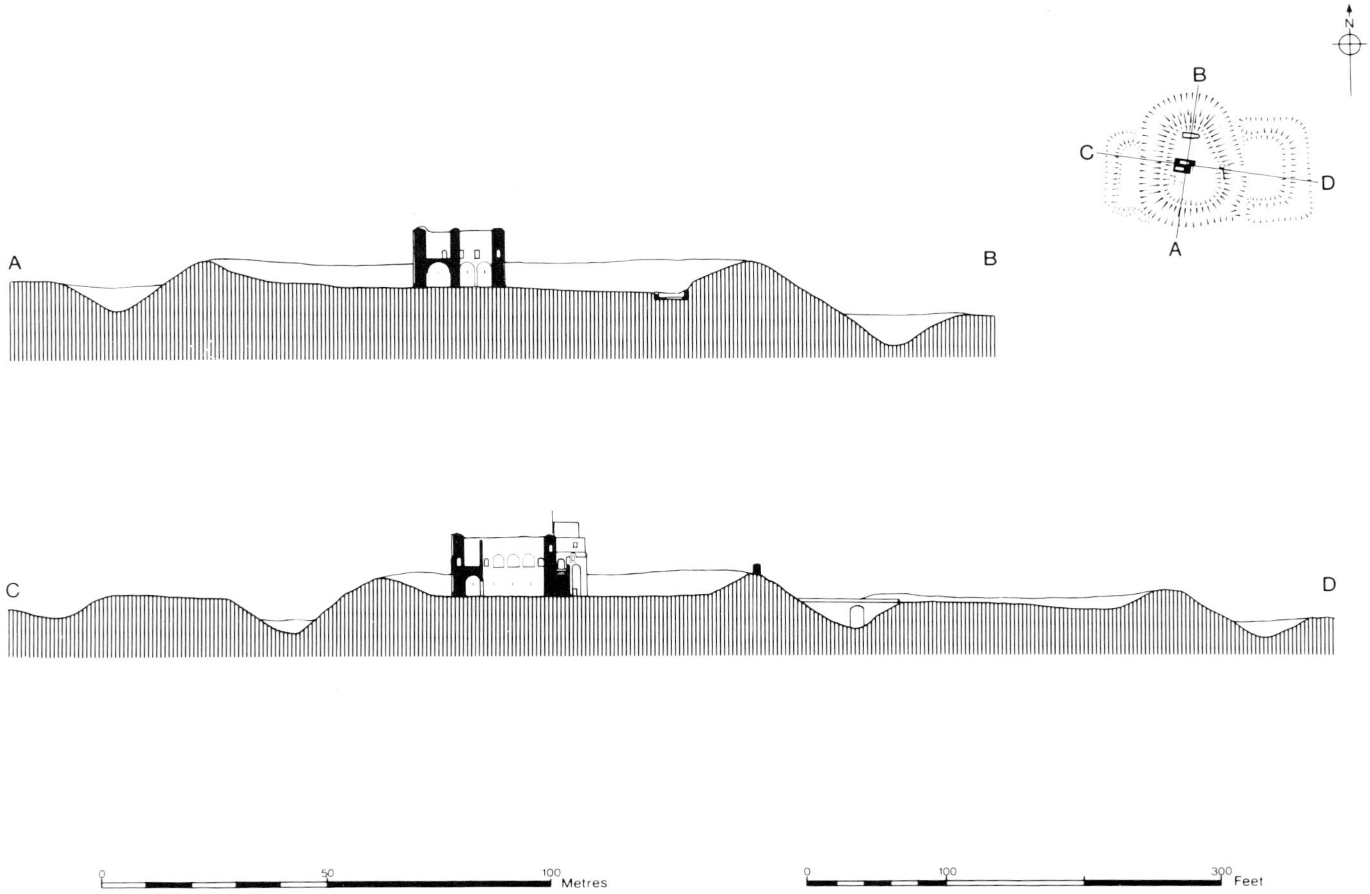

Sections through the site

outer western enclosure), belong exclusively to the castle and to the period after the Norman Conquest. Everything that visitors see is part of the Norman castle and its later development, except the early church by the north bank of the inner enclosure or inner bailey. This, though it contains in its fabric much re-used Roman material of unknown provenance, dates from the later eleventh century and probably the post-Conquest period, and is thus earlier than the castle which has engulfed it, but not by much. Investigation has revealed no trace of any preceding church on the same site. The present ruined fabric (described on page 31) goes with the Saxo-Norman occupation material found in association with it—and also beneath the keep, where there were also traces of Roman occupation material—and has the appearance, from its tripartite division, of having been an early parish church rather than a chapel as it has been previously described.

What happened, it seems, is that when the castle was founded in the early twelfth century the existing and Anglo-Saxon settlement on the site, including the parish church which then became enclosed with the castle bank inconveniently close to it, had to be moved further north to where the village now stands. The modern village shows traces of having been laid out as an exercise in early medieval town-planning [Paul Rutledge, Norwich City Museum, unpublished paper] and it contains the splendid twelfth-century church of St Lawrence, probably begun a little before the keep and evidently the grander replacement of the parish church swallowed up by the castle. The nave is more or less contemporary with the keep, and the west front about a generation later.

While the eastern rectangular outwork, which must always have served, presumably from the beginning, as a barbican defending the main approach and entrance to the castle, has not yet been investigated, the archaeological evidence so far does not conflict with the simplest hypothesis, namely that the whole castle was originally laid out in the form of three enclosures—one central inner bailey and two outer baileys—as it is now. The pattern of history—that is, literary and documentary evidence—points to this foundation as having been in about 1138 by the second generation in England of the family of Albini, a date and occasion which in turn is confirmed by the date of the present parish church at Rising, necessarily built in association with the castle.

Meanwhile the recent archaeological investigations have also revealed certain complications and later alterations to the earthworks. A section immediately north of the ancient ruined church in the inner bailey not only showed finally that the rampart there now is later than the church, against which it abutted and which it shamelessly used as a revetment, but also that it contains within itself another lower and lesser bank, earlier than the present rampart though also later than the church and a little further away from it. In other words, here, and thus presumably all round the inner bailey, the original bank had been substantially heightened and the ditch deepened at some subsequent stage. In addition, investigation of the western outer bailey showed that while this had originally been enclosed by a bank (and ditch) similar in construction to the original and first bank (and ditch) of the inner bailey, at some subsequent date the whole of this western enclosure so formed had been levelled up, to form the kind of quasi-platform that it now is, by dumping large quantities of earth and spoil of a type that might be expected to come from the bottom level of the present great central ditch.

The suggestion is that this (otherwise not easily explained) levelling up of the western outer bailey took place at the same time as, and as part and result of, the major work of deepening the inner ditch and heightening the inner bank. Furthermore, certain archaeological evidence, notably half of a silver penny of the type current between 1158 and 1180 (cut for use as a ha'penny), found on the original surface level of the western outer bailey—that is, beneath the dumping—suggests a date in the late twelfth century for the work. Such a date may seem surprising, and may perhaps suggest the urgency of war, since the substantial heightening of the inner banks to their present level seriously detracts from the lordly dominance which the great keep was undoubtedly intended to have over the township and surrounding land, at a time when such symbolism still mattered, while no trace has yet been found of any late twelfth- or early thirteenth-century curtain wall such as might be expected to have crowned and strengthened their summit (the existing curtain wall, of which fragments and traces remain, is much later—see pages 30-1).

However this may be, there is no doubt that Castle Rising was first founded by the Norman Albini lords of Rising, and little doubt that this was done in their second generation in England and in the person of William de Albini II, soon to be Earl of Sussex, in or very soon after 1138.

Domesday Book (1086) shows that in the eleventh century, both before and after 1066, Rising was a mere 'berewick' or outlying member of the great manor of Snettisham—a fact which itself may argue against any great lordly residence here at that time. As such it had been held by Stigand, the notorious Archbishop of Canterbury from 1052 until his deposition by the Normans in 1070, and thereafter had been granted by the Conqueror to his half-brother Odo, Bishop of Bayeux and Earl of Kent in England. The early church, therefore, now in the inner bailey of the castle, is presumably to be attributed to either of these two in the sense that it was built in the time of one or other of them.

Bishop Odo, though himself in disgrace in the later years of the Conqueror's reign, held Snettisham, with Rising, off and on until his final fall in 1088, soon after the succession of William Rufus which he had opposed. Some time after that the manor of Snettisham and Rising, with the hundreds of Freebridge and Smithdon and a half-share of the customs and tolls (the 'tolbooth') of Lynn, were given by Rufus to the newly arrived William de Albini, which grant was subsequently confirmed by Henry I, though this time in inheritance. We do not

Plate 2 Wymondham Abbey Church from the north, 1947

yet, however, have to suppose the foundation of the castle by the new lord of Rising, for William de Albini also at this time became lord of Buckenham (Norfolk) where there is the impressive site of an early castle attributable to him (see page 10), and which evidently became his principal seat, and the head or *caput* of his Norfolk lands which afterwards were known as the honor of Buckenham. As late as 1243, when the Albini inheritance was divided (see page 16), Buckenham went to the eldest heir as the original patrimony.

The family of Albini or Aubigny, of which more than one branch was to be established in England as the result of the Norman Conquest, came from St-Martin d'Aubigny in Normandy, in the district of the Cotentin and the diocese of Coutances. The first member of the house of whom we have record is one William, lord of St-Martin d'Aubigny, who is known to have married a sister of Grimald du Plessis before 1047—in which year Grimald was disinherited for having fought in the battle of Val-ès-Dunes against the young Duke William, the future Conqueror, and his castle of Le Plessis-Grimoult was confiscated and slighted. This William de Albini was also a benefactor, in association with his son Roger, of the neighbouring abbey of Lessay, founded in 1056. Roger, who was evidently the eldest son and heir, and thus secure in his patrimony, is not known to have crossed to England in or after 1066, though it is likely that he had two younger brothers who did, namely Nigel, who appears as a tenantin-chief at Cainhoe and elsewhere in Bedfordshire in Domesday Book (and is thus the founder of the line of Albini of Cainhoe), and Richard, who became abbot of St Albans from 1097 until his death in 1119. Roger de Albini himself made a grant of property to the abbey of Lessay by a charter dated 1084, in which his son, Rualoc, is associated with him. He had a wife called Amice, who may have been the aunt of Robert de Mowbray, whose lands and honours in Normandy the Albinis were later to acquire. Of Rualoc no more is heard and he is thought to have died early without heirs, but two other sons of Roger de Albini, namely William (the elder of the two) and Nigel, came to England, evidently in the time of Rufus. Both did extremely well for themselves here as fortunate backers of the winning side, supporting both Rufus and Henry I in turn against their elder brother, Robert Curthose, for the Conqueror's inheritance in England and ultimately in Normandy as well. Nigel, who died in 1129, obtained among other things both the wife and Norman lands of Robert de Mowbray, former Earl of Northumberland and broken in 1095. He also obtained the lands in northern England of Robert de Stuteville some time after the latter's fall in 1106. Through his son, Roger, who took the name of Mowbray, he became the founder of the historic house of Mowbray.

William de Albini (known to English genealogists as William de Albini I, though in fact the second of that name) was established in Norfolk especially, where he was granted Snettisham with Rising by both Rufus and Henry I; he was lord of Buckenham, which evidently became the centre of his new honor or barony, and received from the latter King, according to the inquest of 1166, a total of forty-two knights' fees. He stood particularly close to Henry I who gave him the office of butler (hence he is often called, then and now, William de Albini *Pincerna*) and also gave him in marriage Maud, a daughter of the great East Anglian house of Bigod (subsequently Earls of Norfolk), when that young lady was in the King's wardship. He had, in short, arrived, and appropriately, according to the custom of the time, in 1107 he set about founding a religious house as a symbol of his status and the means to obtain heavenly benefits and divine grace and favour for himself, his family and descendants. This was a house for Benedictine monks at Wymondham, not far from his castle of Buckenham. At first it was a priory and a dependency of St Albans (where William's uncle, Richard, was abbot); eventually it became an independent abbey but not until 1449.

Part of the great church, west of the crossing, still stands as the parish church of Wymondham (Plate 2); a grand though fragmentary witness to the rise of Albini. Yet also it is a silent witness unless visitors will look and think and read, for the tombs of William and his successors, the Albini Earls of Sussex, buried before the high altar in their time, are lost now outside in the grass and nettles which grow over the former east end—

development of the rectangular keep, and as such belonging to the turn of the twelfth and thirteenth centuries. It also means that two major castles were thus raised during the so-called 'Anarchy' of Stephen's reign (1135–54). They, with many other instances, give the lie to the curious yet lingering idea that such things could not be done in the circumstances of that troubled period, and even that there is among castles a separate and distinct category to be known as 'the Castles of the Anarchy.'

At present neither the exact appearance nor all the details are known of the castle at Rising as founded in about 1138 by the first Albini Earl of Sussex. It is best to assume all three enclosures, with the western outer enclosure (which now, at least, has no obvious communication with the inner bailey) facing in the direction of the old road from Lynn, and the eastern outer bailey defending the main approach to the castle, which then as now passed through it and so, by a stone bridge across the main inner ditch, to the existing gatehouse. Within the inner bailey rose the splendid keep or donjon, containing the principal accommodation and the state apartments of the lord, looking, in spite of fourteenth-century restoration and alteration (pages 40-2) and in spite of later ruination, much as it does at present. But the inner bailey, at least, must also have contained all the additional accommodation required not only by the great itinerant household of the lord earl but also by the several households of his lady, of his sons when they reached the appropriate age, and of visiting magnates, as well as the more modest establishment of his resident constable. These buildings or their latest replacements are listed in the sixteenth-century surveys of the castle in the evening of its history—hall, chambers, chapel, kitchen, buttery, pantry, constable's lodging, stables and the like; one, evidently the chapel because of its orientation, is shown on Millicent's early eighteenth-century view (Plate 3), and this and others have recently been archeologically investigated (see page 33). The old church, too, though put to secular uses, is known to have survived until the banks finally engulfed it sometime after the sixteenth century, to be rediscovered with great excitement in the 1840s.

What are not known at present are the form and type of the castle's enceinte and its outer defences. It is evident that the bank and ditch of the inner bailey were greatly strengthened and enlarged at a date which seems to have been about 1200 and when the western outer bailey was levelled up to a platform (page 9). Whether the original banks or its present great successor (or the banks of the outer enclosures) were from their beginning crowned with the stone curtain wall one would expect in a castle of this distinction is not yet known. The alternative would be a timber palisade, which may seem an anticlimax in relation to the sophistication of the keep, and in any case the banks would presumably have required revetment because of the shifting nature of the sandy soil. The surviving fragment of brick curtain wall immediately south of the gatehouse dates from the late fourteenth century, and while the footings of a wall can be traced in the turf all round the inner bailey, the only section so far to have been investigated (north of the ancient church) showed itself to be an even later rebuilding.

There is a tradition recorded by the older antiquaries that the three mural towers of the castle were respectively attached to the manors of Hunstanton, Roydon and Wootton, whose lords owed the feudal service of castleguard in them. If this could be proved, it would carry the towers, which were presumably stone, and therefore the wall, back to the earliest period—though there would still be the complication of the heightening of the bank to contend with. Unfortunately no supporting evidence has been found in the documents studied, though the reference in a survey of 1503–06 (page 25) to the service of repairing the battlements of the castle, owed by certain tenants of the lord of Rising, may equally argue for a curtain wall of early date. One of the three mural towers of tradition is shown, ruined and leaning, in the Buck engraving of 1738 (Plate 1); it appears as illustrated to have features of an earlier date than the surviving late-fourteenth-century curtain. It may also be significant that if (which is not certain) the Nightingale Tower mentioned in the survey of 1503–06 (page 25) is a mural tower, a Nightingale Tower is also mentioned in the Black Prince's Register as having been repaired in 1365, and thus must be earlier again than the existing curtain.

Though the times were out of joint, William de Albini II, the founder of Castle Rising, was able to retain the eminence which his marriage to Alice the Queen had brought him. He and his wife are said to have received at Arundel Stephen's rival, the Empress Mathilda, daughter of Henry I, when she first landed in England in 1139, but otherwise they remained loyal to the King. He was instrumental in bringing about the treaty between Stephen and the future Henry II (son of the Empress) which ended the civil war in 1153, and was thereafter prominent in the favour and counsels of the latter King, being employed by him in the controversy with Becket, and serving in arms against the King's rebellious son in 1173–74, in Normandy and in England at the battle of Fornham St Genevieve, near Bury St Edmunds, where the rebel forces of the Earl of Leicester and the Bigod Earl of Norfolk (Albini's neighbour) were defeated. He died in 1176, twenty-five years after the wife who had brought him such good fortune. In 1150 she had withdrawn to the nunnery at Afflighem in her native Brabant, where she died in 1151. He was buried beside his father and his mother before the high altar of their priory church at Wymondham, where all his Albini successors as Earls of Sussex were also to be laid to rest.

The house of Albini continued as Earls of Sussex and lords of Arundel, Rising and Buckenham until 1243. William de Albini III, son and heir of William II, married another widow, this time the former wife of Roger de Clare, thus establishing a connection with an East Anglian baronial family even greater than the Bigod Earls of Norfolk. He died in 1193 and was succeeded by William IV, his son and heir, who married Mabel, daughter of the Earl of Chester, and stood as close to King John as his grandfather had to Henry II.

He was with the King at Runnymede, and surviving from the wars that followed there is a royal writ, dated at Colchester on 24 March 1216, ordering the sheriff of Norfolk and Suffolk to make timber available to the constable of Rising 'to fortify the castle of the Earl of Arundel.' The earl went over to the rebel cause in the June of that same year, but returned to the allegiance of the boy King Henry III in July 1217. Thereafter he went on crusade and was present at the fall of Damietta in 1219, but died on his way home, near Rome in 1221.

From this time onward ill fortune in the guise of death brought the lordship of Albini to an end. William V was evidently just of age in 1221 to succeed his father, but died three years later without an heir and probably unmarried. He was succeeded therefore, by his brother, Hugh, then a boy of nine. Hugh was given seisin of his great possessions (though still under age) in 1235, having married in the previous year Isabel, daughter of William de Warenne, Earl of Surrey and lord of Castle Acre (not far from Castle Rising) in Norfolk. He died, 'in the flower of his youth' on 7 May 1243, again leaving no heirs, and the Albini inheritance was divided among his sisters and co-heiresses, passing in effect to their husbands. Hugh's widow survived him for almost forty years, and was buried in 1282 at Marham, Norfolk, in the church of the convent for Cistercian nuns which she had founded there. Meanwhile by letters patent of 27 November 1243, Buckenham went to Robert de Tatteshall, who had married Mathilda, eldest of the sisters, Arundel to John fitz Alan in right of his wife Isabel, other lands and lordships to Roger de Somery in the right of Nichola, and Castle Rising passed to Roger de Montalt as the inheritance of his wife Cecily, youngest of the co-heiresses.

'Never glad, confident morning again' and in some ways, perhaps, the post-Albini history of Rising may seem an anti-climax after the splendours that had gone before. The house of Montalt, alias Mohaut, was of course distinguished. They had been hereditary stewards of the Earls of Chester from a date soon after the Conquest, and they were lords of the castles of Mold (from which they took their name, de Mohaut, de Monte Alto) and Hawarden. Dugdale, following Matthew Paris, places Roger de Montalt, who succeeded to Castle Rising in 1243, among the greatest barons of the realm in 1250 when he took the Cross to follow St Louis to the Holy Land. Yet they were not earls, the great Albini inheritance which formerly supported Rising had been divided, and their lordship there ended by the sale, in effect, of all their property to the Crown. The quasi-royal possession which then followed, and lasted to the sixteenth century, brought splendours of its own, but it also meant in practice first Isabella, another queen and dowager but also a widow in a world of men, and thereafter the Black Prince and his successors as Dukes of Cornwall, for whom Castle Rising was but one of very many residences, and for whose officials (who had the management of it) it was a 'foreign manor', outside the duchy's lands and lordships in Cornwall and Devon. There were, it is true, substantial works carried out on the keep in this later medieval period, at a date most probably in the early fourteenth century (as well as others later still upon the curtain wall and other buildings—pages 19-20); but while these included the positive work of the heightening of the forebuilding tower by the addition of its present top storey and the vaulting of the entrance vestibule (page 42), they also included the more negative undertaking of restoring and rebuilding the upper levels of the keep itself in such a way as to imply a long period of former neglect and structural decay (pages 40-2).

That decay cannot be dated, and nor, with any precision, can the restoration which followed it, there being no documentary and very little stylistic evidence, though the manner of its execution and certain features (e.g. the figurehead corbels marking a new roof to hall and chamber, the quadrant corbels in the north wall head, the inserted doorway between chamber and chapel—pages 40-2) suggest the earlier fourteenth century. Moreover, it is not unlikely that these reparations were carried out at the same time as the work upon the forebuilding tower, and that can be more securely dated to the period, let us say, of about 1280 to 1320, by the naturalistic foliage of the corbels of the vestibule vault (page 46). If, therefore, we seek a historical pattern to match the overall structural evidence, neglect and decay of the keep at least in the earlier Montalt period after 1243 (Roger, who acquired Castle Rising, is said to have died in poverty) followed by restoration with alteration in the early fourteenth century, may seem an acceptable hypothesis. In such a case it may further be suggested that the most likely candidate to have undertaken the substantial work of renovation is the last of the Montalts, Robert, who was lord of Rising from 1299 to 1329. He was a prominent figure, not least in the wars in Gascony and Scotland, under both Edward I and Edward II, and a magnate close to the court. He was also active in royal affairs in Norfolk, which implies residence in these parts; so, too, does his choice of burial place: not Wymondham where the Albinis lay, but at Shouldham Priory, also in Norfolk and not far from Rising—as his wife too, Emma de Stradsett (Norfolk), was buried nearby in the church at Stradsett, where Blomefield, the Norfolk historian, formerly noted her epitaph.

The only memorable event recorded touching the Montalt lordship at Rising from 1243 to 1331 is a great law-suit in the Court of King's Bench in 1313, between Robert de Montalt and the Mayor and Commonalty of Lynn, brought about by a fracas between them in the town, itself occasioned by a dispute over the lord of Rising's share of the tolbooth and customs of Lynn, and resulting in a very heavy payment of compensation to Robert. The deed whereby this Robert, the last of his line, in effect conveyed Rising to the Crown for the sum of 10 000 marks (£6666-13s-4d) is in the form of letters patent dated 8 April 1327, enrolled upon the Patent Rolls where it still survives. By it Robert de Montalt and Emma (de Stradsett) his wife were licensed to enfeoff Master Henry de Clif, king's clerk (a mere agent in the matter) with the castle and manor of Rising and appurtenances, including their share of the tolbooth of

Lynn, with their other properties, including the castle and manors of Mold and Hawarden and the stewardship of Chester; the said Master Henry to convey them back again to Robert and Emma and the heirs of Robert, but with successive remainders to Isabella the Queen Mother for life, John of Eltham, brother to the King, Edward III, in tail, and ultimately to the King himself and his heirs. Two years later, in 1329, Robert de Montalt died without issue (that clause of the letters patent being evidently a formality), and two years after that his widow, Emma, surrendered her remaining rights in Castle Rising to Queen Isabella for an annuity of £400 a year. This was in 1331, and in the winter of 1331–32 Emma died.

In 1331 Isabella, 'the She-Wolf of France' and former paramour of Mortimer (and thus the principal accomplice in both the deposition and the murder in 1327 of Edward II, her husband) entered into possession of Castle Rising and retained it until her death in 1358. This is the best-known phase and the only popularly known fact in the history of the castle, though badly bent by legend.

In no sense did the formidable Isabella languish as a prisoner at Rising during those twenty-seven years, nor was she even socially in disgrace. The façade of monarchy must remain untarnished, the cracks be papered over, the scandal suppressed. Thus Isabella measured out her days like any other dowager queen, amply endowed with revenues and lands worth £3000 a year (great wealth in the money of the time), moving with her retinue and household from one residence to another like any other great lady of the age, and, doubtless, every inch a queen. Her residences included the former Montalt castles of Mold and Hawarden (both subsequently sold) and the castles of Mere, in Wiltshire, and Hertford as well as Rising. Nevertheless there is plentiful evidence of Isabella's frequent and prolonged presence at Castle Rising, notably in the Lynn Chamberlain's accounts where it takes the form of politic presents and other expenses of neighbouring majesty ('Also for 2 shillings for the carts to carry the Queen's luggage. . . Also. . . for 20s given for bread sent to Isabella the Queen Dowager when she came from Walsingham. . . Also for £4-3s-4d given for a cask of wine sent to her'—1331). There is evidence there also, and upon the Chancery rolls, of royal visits to the Queen Mother at Rising by Edward III, her son (not the least important feature of whose brilliant and victorious kingship was domestic peace), with Philippa his Queen and their court and households as, for example, in 1342, 1343, 1344 and 1349. On one such occasion the long-suffering mayor of Lynn was commanded to send eight carpenters to prepare the castle for the King's coming.

Excavations south of the keep in recent years have revealed traces of stone buildings erected at about the time of Isabella's arrival at the castle (see page 21). They seem to form a residential suite with rooms progressing from a main hall via a covered passage to a first-floor lodging in a western block. At right angles to this latter range lay the building long recognised as a chapel, its masonry now once more repaired and visible. At its west end was evidence to suggest a gallery. This would have been reached from the first-floor lodging, allowing services to be watched in privacy. It is tempting to see the suite as a whole as accommodation for Isabella herself, from audience chamber to inner closet, leaving the refurbished rooms in the keep for formal and ceremonial use only. Details of a possible further range linking this accommodation directly with the door to the keep were lost in the nineteenth-century clearance of the bailey. Further to the east, beyond where the oak tree stands now, a great brick kitchen was built, with a number of ancillary service buildings. Archaeology, as a discipline, deals with what societies leave behind. A well-ordered medieval household, as the Dowager Queen's clearly was, leaves little in the way of artifacts to shed light on its daily life. Thus the excavations have nothing to add to the bare facts presented by the documents; no insight into either the household's everyday routines or the pageantry of the King's visits.

These, then, were great days again at Rising, and one would give much to have observed them. And when the captains and Kings departed, the eagles and the trumpets, one may wonder what the ageing Isabella thought about, as she sat—perhaps by those windows in the keep, where visitors may now stand—and her son waged war in France. Did she marvel how she, with his useless father, Edward of Caernarfon now laid in pious state in his sumptuous tomb at Gloucester, could ever have conceived him? She died, not at Rising but in her castle at Hertford, on 23 August 1358. The gold in the chest in her closet was counted up (£311-10s—PRO Exchequer, Accounts Various, 393/5, f11), her household paid off and dismissed, and Castle Rising passed to her grandson, the Black Prince. She was buried in the church of the Grey Friars by Newgate in London, and Edward III, her son, dutiful to the end, ordered the streets of the city to be cleansed for her last passing.

In 1337, by charter dated 1 October and enrolled upon the Charter Rolls, and following the death of John of Eltham, Earl of Cornwall and the first reversioner, the previous year, Edward III, as King and residuary legatee, had altered the terms of the original Montalt conveyance ten years before, and granted the castle and manor of Rising, with its valuable appurtenance of one quarter of the tolbooth of Lynn, to Edward his eldest son, new created Duke of Cornwall, to take effect after the death of Isabella. The charter is entirely explicit that Castle Rising is thus to be attached to the Duchy of Cornwall in perpetuity, and not to be alienated, reverting to the Crown, like the Duchy itself, only in the temporary circumstance of the absence of a son and heir to the reigning monarch. In 1358, therefore, the Black Prince, aged twenty-eight, entered into possession of Castle Rising—or rather, added it to his vast possessions—and retained it until his untimely death in 1376.

It is likely that the brick curtain wall of which a short section survives (page 30) immediately south of the gatehouse (itself modified, perhaps at this date—page 29) belongs to the Black Prince's time, and though there is no documentary evidence for this supposition there is for certain other works then put in hand. The *Black Prince's Register* (HMSO, iv (1933), page 346) contains an instrument dated March 1360, whereby the Prince 'being anxious that the bridge outside the gates of his castle of Rising, and any other defects there, should be speedily repaired in view of the multitude of perils which might easily befall the castle in these present times,' gives notice that he has appointed his receiver at Rising, Philip Pyncheon, to take carpenters and other workmen, with transport for timber and other materials, to repair the same; while another letter informs the receiver that the Prince has requested the Bishop of Norwich to let him have a dozen oaks for the work. These things, it is noted, are done by the advice of the Bishop of Winchester, William of Wykeham, at this time Clerk of the King's Works and in charge of great royal works at Windsor and elsewhere. The Prince's register also contains (iv, 463) what is evidently a standing order of 1362 authorising the same Philip, receiver at Rising, to repair as necessary from time to time any defects in 'the houses of the prince's castle there'—that is, the miscellaneous buildings within the castle enclosure, which may or may not include the keep.

Most interesting of all, perhaps, though enigmatic, is an instrument of 1365 (*ibid*, page 559) ordering the auditors of Philip Pyncheon's account to credit him with the sum of £81-1s-2d spent by him, by order of the prince's council, on 'the repair of the tower Called Nightegale in the Castle of Rising, as more fully appears by an indenture. . .enclosed.' Unfortunately that indenture giving details is not known to have survived, and the Nightingale Tower cannot be identified with any confidence. A 'Nyghtyngall Towre' is mentioned again in a survey of the castle taken in about 1503–06 (page 25), where it at least is evidently not the great tower or keep—though it might be the present gate-tower, or the 'old tower by the gate-house' mentioned in the survey of 1542–43 (page 26). If it could be identified as a mural tower other than the gatehouse, then the fact that it was being repaired, not built, in the Black Prince's time would be of importance in relation to the problem of the outer defences of the castle in the earlier period (page 15).

It would appear, therefore, that at the time of the Black Prince's death in 1376 Castle Rising was in good structural order, and there is evidence that in the late fourteenth century, with the threat of raids and invasion from France, it was regarded as defensible and several times put in a state of defence. It is possible, therefore, that the two early cannon, formerly to be seen here but at present on display in the Tower of London, pertain to this period. In 1377, Castle Rising then being in the King's hands, the constable was instructed not to exact from the Prior of Westacre, on the strength of a royal commission to compel all tenants of the castle to perform the services they owed, a watch of sixteen men every night there at the prior's own cost, since the convent 'holds no lands of the King or castle or of the King's lordship there, and ought not to do any service towards the ward thereof.' In 1385 and again in 1386 the

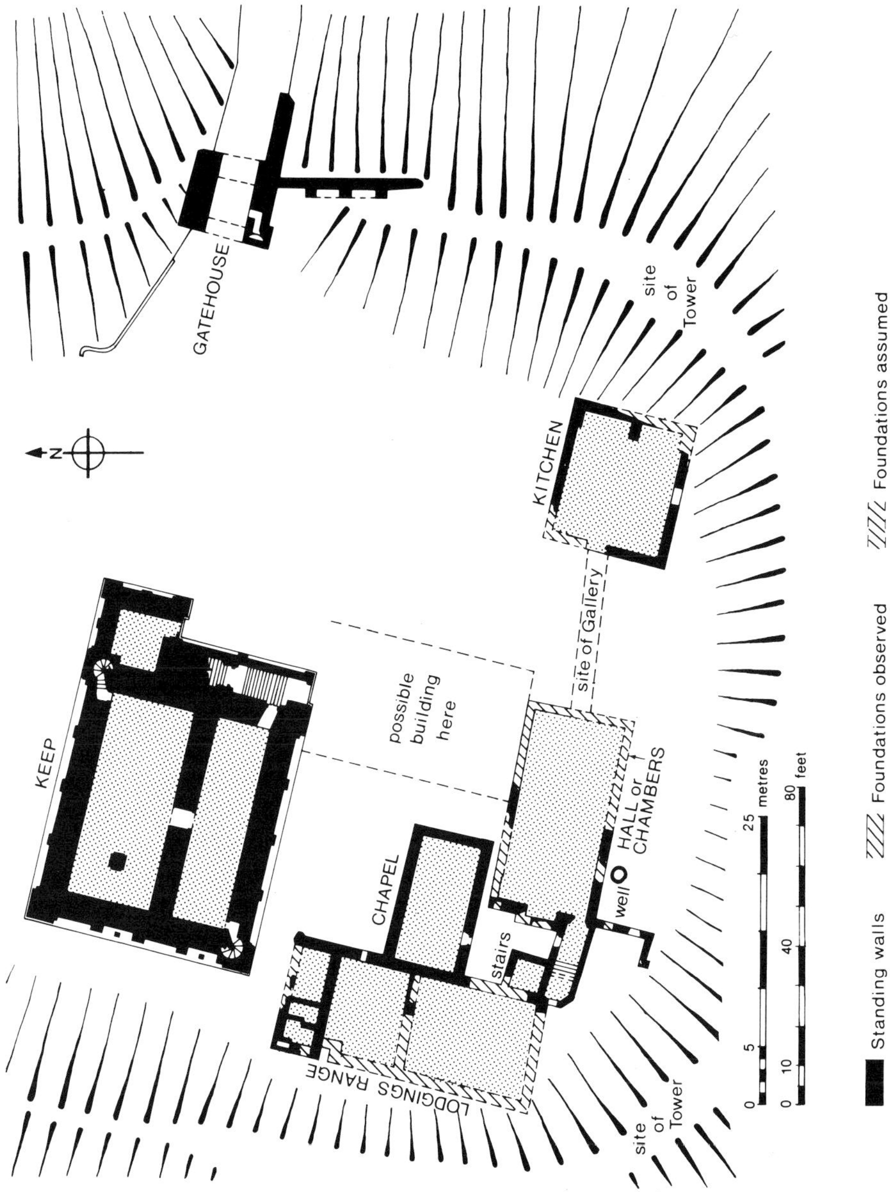

N
KEEP
GATEHOUSE
CHAPEL
possible building here
site of Gallery
KITCHEN
site of Tower
HALL or CHAMBERS
well
stairs
LODGINGS RANGE
site of Tower
0 5 10 25 metres
0 10 40 80 feet
Standing walls
Foundations observed
Foundations assumed

Site plan

constable was further commissioned 'to compel as he thinks fit the men of the parts near the castle to abide in it upon its safe custody whenever any danger of invasion or attack is imminent, as in times past;' and in the latter year a commission of array to Richard Fodryngay as constable specifies the danger as 'Charles, King of France, who is reported to be about to invade England.'

Nevertheless, it was during these years also that the new King, Richard II, having no son and heir and thus holding the Duchy of Cornwall himself, three times alienated the castle and its appurtenances in spite of the terms of Edward III's charter of 1337. In 1378 he, or the councillors of his minority, exchanged it for the castle of Brest with John, Duke of Brittany, the husband of the King's sister, Joan, and Duke John was thus the (largely absentee) lord of Rising—valued at £110 a year over and above the cost of maintenance—until 30 June 1397. Meanwhile in 1386 the reversion of it was granted to the King's uncle, Thomas, Duke of Gloucester, though that conveyance proved abortive on his forefeiture and death in 1397. Thereafter and in the same year, Richard II granted Rising in tail to another uncle, Edmund, Duke of York, which grant was renewed in 1399 by Henry IV after Richard's deposition.

Soon afterwards, however, these several alienations were declared illegal and Castle Rising reverted to the Duchy of Cornwall where it properly belonged. Thus in 1402 Edward, son and heir of Edmund late Duke of York, was granted livery of his inheritance except for the castle and lordship of Rising, about which a suit in Chancery was said to be pending between him and Henry the King's son and Prince of Wales—i.e. Henry of Monmouth, then also Duke of Cornwall. Prince Hal won his suit and recovered his castle and lordship, with one quarter of the tolbooth of Lynn and all other appurtenances. The judges in Chancery declared that the alienations of Richard II and Henry IV after him were out of order by the terms of the charter of Edward III, duly recited, it manifestly having been that monarch's will 'for ever to annexe [them] to the Duchy of Cornwall so that they should never be severed from it, nor by him or his heirs be given or granted to any others than the Dukes of Cornwall.' Thus even the King 'may not and ought not to' give them to anyone else. In terms of historical interest at least, on the double grounds of this decision and the charter of 1337, the final alienation by Henry VIII in 1544 was no less out of order than the alienations of his late-fourteenth century predecessors, and it is remarkable that it has never been quashed or revoked.

From 1403 until 1544 Castle Rising remained a part of the Duchy of Cornwall, held by the Duke and Prince when there was one, and by the King himself when there was not. In 1461, at the height of the Wars of the Roses, when the Yorkist Edward IV was about to displace the Lancastrian Henry VI, the castle was once more put in a state of defence, the escheator in Norfolk being ordered to take it over in the King's name and place sufficient men-at-arms therein to guard it. Yet in the main this must have been, at least towards its end, the period of the castle's decline, and it is thus frustrating that it should also be the period for which we have the most documentary evidence about it. Nevertheless, the Ministers' and Bailiff's Accounts and the several surveys which survive from the fifteenth and sixteenth centuries, though they record for the most part only minor repairs, are of importance in showing that the place was maintained in some sort until 1544 at least, while by their incidental references to them they provide useful information about its various components and appurtenances towards the end of its long history.

Thus, in addition to small sums spent upon various unspecified 'houses' and chambers within the castle, there are similar references to 'a certain chamber at the gate . . . called le Foster Chaumber' in 1452–53, to the making good 'of part of the stone wall totally collapsed in the east part of the castle next the gate' in 1528–29 (though only 34s 4d seems to have been spent upon it by the bailiff), and to the repair of 'the great gates' themselves in 1530–31. The bridge at the entrance to the castle frequently received attention, in 1454–55 the actual reference being to 'the making (*factura*) of the castle bridge there,' though the sum entered on the account is only 66s 10d. In 1531–32 there was work upon the kitchen among other 'houses within the castle,' and in the previous year something called the *magnum erreum* was repaired, as it had been also in

Plate 4 Engraving of the castle by T Hearne, 1782

1454–55. The *erreum* must have some connection with birds, and may be the dovecote (ever a sign and privilege of lordship in the Middle Ages) which is referred to in other years. The stables and grange are mentioned and, among the appurtenances of castle and manor, we hear especially of the mills, the warren, and the chase or forest—though no more of the Queen's garden of Isabella's time.

Rising Chase, reported at one time to have had a circumference of some 24 miles (39km), had a hunting lodge within it and its own surveyor or ranger in charge. That office was frequently combined with that of constable of the castle, and was held in the fifteenth century by some very eminent personages, including Ralph Lord Cromwell and John de Vere, Earl of Oxford. One may suspect, indeed, that by the Tudor period the hunting which it provided, over and above its useful rents and revenues, was the main attraction of Rising to its lords, and one is reminded of a letter of 1538, still surviving among the State Papers, from the Duke of Norfolk to the Duke of Suffolk, 'written upon a molehill in Rysnyg Chase, 8 August, 11 o'clock.'

There were other distinguished visitors to the castle in these years. A letter of 'Mary, Queen of France' to Wolsey survives, dated at Rising on 17 March 1528. This was Mary, sister of Henry VIII, married first to the old King Louis of France and then, released by his death shortly after, making a love match in 1515 with Charles Brandon, Duke of Suffolk and the King's favourite, in almost the only Tudor romance with a happy ending. Another letter similarly survives to Wolsey from the same Charles Brandon, dated at Rising on 24 March 1530. Castle Rising thus remained a scene and setting for gracious living and the Beautiful People of the age, and it cannot have ceased to be so when in 1544 Henry VIII granted the castle, manor and chase (though evidently not the lucrative tolbooth at Lynn), with the manors of Gaywood and Thorpe (formerly belonging to the Bishop of Norwich), to Thomas Howard, Duke of Norfolk, and Henry, Earl of Surrey, his son and heir, in exchange for Walton, Trimley, Falkenham and other Suffolk lands of theirs, formerly belonging to Felixstowe priory. One wonders what suitable accommodation these lords and their ladies found at Rising when the surviving surveys of the late fifteenth and sixteenth centuries speak mostly of dilapidation and decay, and the answer is presumably the 'new loggyng' mentioned in the survey of 1542–43, with its kitchen, larder house, chapel, 'other houses necessary,' and its 'long stable.' Indeed it may be this 'new loggyinge' which has been located by excavation south of the keep; a rebuilding in brick and timber framing, of the lodging of Isabella's time mentioned earlier.

We must turn finally to the surveys, all of them printed by Henry Harrod (*Norfolk Archaeology*, iv (1855), 85*ff*), the Norfolk historian, and all or most of them still surviving among Augmentation and Exchequer records at the Public Record Office. The first, from the 1480s (surely misdated by Harrod as 21 Edward III), mentions only the great barn 'which is in grete decaye,' the chase with the deer therein, and the warren, which needs restoring—for 'now there is as much Wermyn in as Conyes.' The next survey (i.e. 'C'), dated 1482–83 by Harrod, deals mainly with the mills pertaining to the manor, of which there were then five, one a fulling mill. For the castle, it confines itself to one pessimistic sentence: 'As towchyng the reparacions of the Castell, yt ys in such decaye that £100 wold lytyll be sene in reparyng of yt, for there ys never a howse abyll to kepe owt the reyne water, wynde, nor snowe.'

The third survey ('D' in Harrod) dates evidently from 1503–06 and is much more informative. Having first stated that the castle is 'evyll repayred,' the commissioners go on to report that certain reparations had recently been begun but not finished, and that they will be wasted if they are not completed. These works were upon the porter's lodge, the constable's lodging, the Nightingale Tower, the hall and great chamber with the gallery between them, the chapel, kitchen, buttery and pantry. Of these, the porter's lodge is presumably to be associated with the gatehouse, the position of the constable's lodging is unknown, and the Nightingale Tower was mentioned before in the Black Prince's time (page 20). For the rest, the hall, great chamber and connecting gallery or covered way, the chapel, the kitchen, buttery and pantry, are the regular components of a lordly residence such as one would expect to find in the inner bailey of Rising or any other castle at almost any date; some or all of them must equate with buildings whose traces were found by excavation south of the keep. The western range was retained from Isabella's time, with its attached chapel. The rest was rebuilt in brick and timber framing, although it has not been possible to identify a kitchen of quite this period. The chapel referred to was of course not the early church now half buried in the bank (page 8) as this evidently lost its sacred use at an early date, and all the buildings listed are additional to the accommodation once afforded by the keep, as that is next dealt with separately in the survey.

The commissioners state that 'the greate Square Towre within the said Castell ys to be loked upon, whether it is better to take downe the Roof and sell it away or not'; they add that it is roofed with tiles, but has 'grete gutters of lede abowt the same.' While, therefore, it is sometimes necessary to take the professional pessimism of surveys with a pinch of salt, the Albini keep or donjon was evidently in a bad way in 1503–06, and was regarded by the surveyors as possibly irreparable—or, rather, not worth repairing. The tiled roof of their report is certainly not original, but may be part of the early fourteenth-century reparation (page 17). The stable within the castle is next listed, as in need of repair to its walls and tiled roof.

Lastly it is reported that the curtain walls about the castle are 'evyll repayred . . . and yf they be not amendyd they will fall downe.' At this point the commissioners add a note of some interest, for they report that it is said that Sir Roger le Strange and the heirs of Sir Henry Heydon are bound by their tenure to repair 'certain cornells' (i.e. battlements or crenellations) of the castle. Such tenurial services are usually of an early date in origin, and may therefore imply that there was a curtain wall (though not the present one) at Castle Rising from the beginning (cf page 15). The survey ends with an estimate of £40 for completing the works (presumably those first listed as already begun, and not the entire restoration of the whole castle) if building materials already there are used, and suggests a sale of timber within and without the chase to raise the sum.

The next survey of Castle Rising was taken in 1542–43 and may perhaps be associated with the impending exchange with the Howards. ('E' in Harrod. The original has not so far been found and the reference Harrod gives is wrong.) It begins with the bald statement that 'the Castell of Rysynge and dyvers houses and walls within and aboute the same bene at this daye in greate ruin and decaye,' and goes on to list as being in that condition the keep ('an olde greate towre or loggyng in soe greate decaye that it passeth our knowledge to exteine the charges to builden; for all the buildings within it and over it is cleane wasted awaye, except the mayne walles'), an old lodging called the old hall, an old tower by the gatehouse, with the gates and bridge, an old house 'called the dungyn' (which evidently, however, is not the keep), and the curtain—that is, 'the outwarde walles of the castell' which 'be soe greatly in decaye that wee thinke to repaire them sufficiently it will cost £100.'

This, however, is also the survey which more cheerfully records the 'new lodging,' already referred to above, all its component buildings of 'late tyme newe repaired in coveringe, glaseinge, and makeings certayne perticions within the same.' The archaeological investigation has shown that at some time in the middle of the century many of the buildings south of the keep were ruthlessly demolished. This left standing only the chapel (with curiously, the adjacent west range latrine block) and the 'new lodging' southeast of it. The transfer to the Howards, following this survey of dilapidations, offers a precise historical context for this clearance. The new lodging survived only a further fifty years before it was itself razed to the ground at the end of the century. Only the chapel stood on, to crumble away over the next three hundred years. What is left is now conserved and visible in the turf.

The 1542–43 survey also covers the chase and the number of beasts within it, and there is reference, in connection with the constableship, to 'a certaine grounde called the Constabulary, neare unto the Castell' which is said to be surrounded by 'a greate olde ditche' part of which is newly raised, and to have a breed of 'conyes' in it pertaining to the constable's office.

The last echo of Castle Rising while it was still, so to speak, alive, and before it became a mere antique ruin, curiosity and ancient monument, comes from the later years of Elizabeth's reign in a survey of the lands and possessions of the Duke of Norfolk then in the Queen's hand following his rebellion and execution in 1572. Now the rabbits predominate, for we are told that 'by encrease of conies suffered by the Wariner, Stephen Bull, to breed in the castell ditches and bancks of the castell in Rising, the same bancks are decayed and the walls are alreadie in part and the rest in danger of overthrowing, if the conyes shall so continue'. The commissioners tartly add that the castle banks and ditches should be no part of the warren, and nor should the constabulary be and has only so been used of late. As for the castle as a whole, they state with an arrogant (and ignorant) contempt that it 'was erected at the first but for speare and shield, and for that force it may be maynteynde if it please her Majestie to be at the charge'. This charge they estimate at £2000. 'And further, if the same castle should be taken downe and sold for benefitt, it is so greatlie decaied as the same will not yeld above one hundred markes' (£66-13s-4d).

Happily Castle Rising was not pulled down, though, increasingly a ruin, its remaining history can be briefly told. From the time of Henry VIII's alienation of it to the Duke of Norfolk in 1544 it has remained in the Howard family until the present day, though passing from the main branch in 1693 when Henry Howard, then Duke of Norfolk, sold it to his kinsman Thomas Howard. There is reference a little after, in 1705, to the taking of stone from the fabric for the repair of a sluice on the estate. (Norwich Record Office, Howard 789 (349×3).) In the nineteenth century much interest in and care of the castle was taken by the Honourable Fulke Greville Howard who had married the heiress Mary and taken the name of Howard in 1807. He was responsible also for the restoration by Salvin of the present parish church which contains his monument, and to him the local historian, William Taylor, dedicated his excellent *History and Antiquities of Castle Rising, Norfolk* in about 1850. In his time 'many thousand loads' of sand and soil eroded from the banks were carted from the inner bailey to get it somewhere near its proper level, the basement of the keep was similarly dug out (this last, at least, in 1822), and 'judicious repairs' were undertaken to preserve the surviving structure of the keep itself. It was during these operations that the ancient chapel or early church was discovered with much excitement, buried in the north bank, and after Fulke Greville Howard's death in 1846 further investigations and excavations were conducted about it by permission of his widow, Mary Howard. The castle site and buildings finally passed into the custody of the State in 1958.

Description

The great earthworks which form the whole site and extent of the castle have already been discussed (page 5). They cover an area of between 12 and 13 acres (4.8 and 5.3km), and comprise a main central enclosure, or inner bailey, and two lesser outworks respectively to east and west. The central enclosure, in shape something between a circle and an oval about 80yd (73m) north to south and 70yd (64m) east to west, has a circumference around its crest of about 350yd (320m), and is far and away the strongest, with its banks, even now after the cumulative and combined effects of erosion and in-filling, rising to a height of some 60ft (18m) from the present bottom of the ditch outside them and some 30ft (9m) from the surface of the bailey within. It is know known, however, that at some stage, apparently in the late twelfth or early thirteenth century, the original banks were considerably heightened to their present size (page 8) and would not in the beginning have so much dwarfed the intended majestic keep they shelter as they have done since. [See the Glossary for an explantion of technical terms.]

The subsidiary eastern enclosure forms an outwork or barbican to the main entrance of the castle across the main ditch and through the gatehouse. It measures some 90 by 65yd (82 by 59m) and its bank and ditch are less formidable (though at some points only just so) than those of the inner bailey. It may possibly be the constabulary of sixteenth-century surveys (and is boldly thus marked on Harrod's conjectural plan of 1855). Whether it was once further strengthened by a curtain wall and whether it contained any buildings of its own is not at present known; it now contains the ticket office.

The western subsidiary enclosure has a bank and ditch, less strong but still considerable, and was levelled up inside, by dumping earth and spoil, presumably from the main inner ditch then being enlarged, to form a kind of platform, again in the late twelfth or early thirteenth century. It provides an outwork in the direction of the old route from Lynn, but is now, at least, cut off from the rest of the castle with which there is no visible interconnection. It, too, may possibly be the constabulary of the later surveys.

Visitors enter the castle from the car park to the south or on foot direct from the village to the north, in either case along the eastern edge of the ditch of the inner bailey and via the eastern enclosure or barbican guarding the original approach. From here one turns across the bridge which spans the main ditch or moat, at this point some 78ft (24m) wide, to the gatehouse.

The bridge, much renewed over the centuries, is now mostly of brick though original stonework can be seen in the piers. It was formerly of two arches, the inner arch now being filled up, beyond which there was probably once a drawbridge pit before the gateway.

Plate 5 Aerial view from the southeast

Gatehouse

The gatehouse itself appears to be basically of the same date as the keep—that is, about 1138—and is of an early type, being in form simply a rectangular tower pierced by the entrance passage with a room above. Much more of it than now survives is shown on the eighteenth-century engraving of the castle by Millicent (Plate 3), where it stands to its full height and is battlemented. The tower is built on the natural ground level with the banks abutting against it on either side. From its outer, eastern, face two straight walls projected one on each side of the entrance, to enclose and defend the approach and thus form a barbican. Only the southern of these two parallel walls survives, with the remains of a staircase in it. This barbican was evidently a later addition, for behind the ruined southern wall, more or less in line with it and itself projecting from the outer face of the gatehouse tower, one can still see the ashlar top of an earlier and original buttress.

Inside the entrance passage, with its plain, semi-circular arches at either end, one can immediately see the grooves or chases for the portcullis, once worked from the chamber above. That chamber and the upper levels of the tower have now gone, but in the two eastern angles, just below first-floor level, one can still see scalloped capitals or corbels which indicate that the entrance passage was once vaulted, though not originally. On either side of the passage there are recesses, two on the north side and one on the south, and also on the south side, at the far end, there is a doorway leading into a newel staircase or vice which gave access to the upper chamber. This staircase is not merely now ruined and

Plate 6 Bridge and gatehouse

blocked, but at some stage has been half cut away to the west, so that it appears that originally the whole gatehouse projected further into the inner bailey than it does now.

Curtain wall

Immediately adjacent to the gatehouse on its south side there remains a short section of curtain wall on the crest of the bank and now leaning inwards. It was constructed with a series of deep recesses or arches on its inner face, which incorporate the shooting embrasures or fish-tail arrow loops and presumably carried the wall-walk above them. This curtain wall is of brick on stone foundations, has a resemblance to sections of the town defences at Lynn but is somewhat crudely constructed, and probably dates from the late fourteenth century. Traces of what appear to be same wall can still be seen in the grass at many points along the crest of the bank about the inner bailey, though the only point so far to be archaeologically investigated, north of the old church, has revealed still later work of brick, with no foundations whatever. This presumably represents some later and ill-executed reparation, and certainly the survey of 1503–06 speaks of the curtain wall as being both 'evyll repayred' and in imminent danger of collapse (page 25).

The Buck view of 1738 (Plate 1) shows more of the curtain wall than now survives and also, southwest of the keep, a shattered and drunkenly leaning fragment of one of the three mural towers traditionally said to have stood at

Plate 7 Early Norman church

intervals about the circuit of the enceinte—the exact positions are at present unknown. The ruined tower as Buck engraved it seems to have features suggesting a much earlier date than the surviving section of fourteenth-century curtain wall, as also it is shown apparently rising from the natural ground level, like the gatehouse, and not from the summit of the bank which carries the existing late-medieval wall. In short, here again is the suggestion that the castle was enclosed from an early date or from the beginning by stone walls and towers as well as by banks and ditches, though present knowledge of its original overall form remains so uncertain as to leave the matter conjectural.

Ancient church

Within the inner bailey the only building, apart from the great keep itself, until recently visible was the ancient church (the so-called chapel) north of the keep and hard against the bank. It was discovered in the early nineteenth century when the bailey was cleared of accumulated sand and soil, and is the earliest building standing on the site, dating in fact from the pre-castle period (page 8). It belongs to the late eleventh century, and is most probably the first parish church of Rising (no trace of any earlier church has been discovered in association with it), necessarily abandoned to be replaced by the present fine twelfth-century church when the castle was founded and enclosed it. Its masonry, somewhat rude in character, differs from that of the keep and incorporates Roman materials including tiles. The alleged herring-bone masonry in it, a feature of most earlier guidebooks, is in fact the remains of a late fireplace inserted in and near the north door at the west end in Tudor times (as, indeed, Harrod noted in 1855).

The building is small, measuring some 42ft (13m) in length internally, including the apsidal east end. It comprises three distinct cells or units, the nave at the west end measuring some 25 by 12ft (7.6 by 3.6m), followed by the slightly narrower and almost square central section (choir or presbytery?) which may conceivably have carried a small central tower, and the apse or chancel. The original floor was at one level throughout, and not raised up at the east end as was formerly thought. What happened was that the whole floor within the church was allowed to rise during the medieval period until it was level with the ground surface of the bailey outside, so that eventually the Tudor fireplace (which is now once more exposed) at the west end was inserted at a floor level then about 3ft (0.9m) above that of the eleventh century.

The nave had two opposing doors at the west end, north and south. There are traces of possible drawbar holes by the north doorway, which is now blocked by nineteenth-century materials, and the south doorway is now partially blocked by the Tudor fireplace. The Victorian antiquaries found, in the course of investigating their discovery, 'the base of the font, 2ft 3in (685mm) square, with an aperture for the drain' (Taylor, *History and Antiquities of Castle Rising,* page 7), between the two doorways at the west end of the nave. It being further discovered that the measurements of this base exactly fitted the measurements of the shaft of the existing font in the present parish church, it was concluded that that shaft, thus still to be seen, is in fact the original font from this preceding church now in the castle. The base having now disappeared, the hypothesis can no longer be tested, but if it is true it strengthens the case for identifying the building containing it as the former parish church.

All round the foot of the walls of the nave there is a low projection or stone bench which is now known to have been of two builds. Originally it was a mere narrow projection of some 6in (150mm), of uncertain purpose, and on the north and south walls only; it was enlarged to its present width, presumably to form a bench, soon after the church was built, and at the same time it was continued at that width all round the nave and into the central section, reducing the width of the archway into the central presbytery in so doing. The south window in the presbytery, recorded in the nineteenth century, has now gone, but two windows—that is, the east window and one to the north—still survive in the apse, each of narrow opening, roundheaded and deeply splayed internally. It is likely that the building ceased to have an ecclesiastical function at or soon after the foundation of the castle and was put to secular uses, and while the first castle bank to the north of it evidently did not block its north door and window the second and larger bank certainly did so and abutted against the whole building (page 8).

Between this ancient church and the keep there is a well (the keep contains another in its basement), and all around the perimeter of the bailey there are traces in the turf of at least the foundations of further buildings. These must be the remains of the many apartments and offices, over and above the accommodation in the keep, required at any date by the large households of the lord of Rising and others periodically visiting the castle (page 14). Some of those to the south of the keep were explored in archaeological excavations in the 1970s. This work included the chapel seen standing in Millicent's early eighteenth-century print (Plate 3) its lower courses now restored to view. It formed part of residential accommodation built in the fourteenth century and brought back into use, after a period of serious decay, in the sixteenth (page 24). On this southern side at least, no trace was found of ancillary buildings of the Norman period.

Keep

The keep (or great tower or donjon) is the finest building in the castle, and was meant to be; it was not only the strongest building but also it contained the best residential accommodation for the Albini lord of Rising. Architecturally, like others of its kind, it both symbolises and embodies lordship, and hence the medieval word for such a place, donjon, derived from Latin *dominium,* meaning lordship. Dating without doubt from about the year 1138 when the young William de Albini II married the Queen of England (page 12) and was made at first Earl of Lincoln and thereafter Earl of Sussex, it belongs to the so-called hall-type of keep. It is not a true tower, the principal dimension of which is verticality—for example, the near-contemporary keep at Castle Hedingham in Essex, or the closely related Rochester in Kent—but a squatter, more oblong edifice, essentially a first-floor hall and chamber(s), strongly built. It is the type of keep found (with further elaborations) at Colchester and the Tower of London, or at Chepstow (Gwent) before its later heightening, or in a literary description of Brionne in Normandy in 1047, and which may well go back to Langeais in Anjou, one of the earliest surviving keeps in Europe, dating from about 994.

The great tower at Rising, also, partly in the degree of its external ornament and more especially in its overall plan and internal arrangements, has particular affinities with the keep at Norwich, which in its final and finished design is attributed to Henry I (1100–35) and itself is related to his keep at Falaise. Rising and Norwich, of course, are close enough geographically to be the product of the same masons and traditions, but it is also just possible that the former owes its similarity to the latter, and to Falaise, to the same Queen Alice, King Henry's widow, whom the second Albini married.

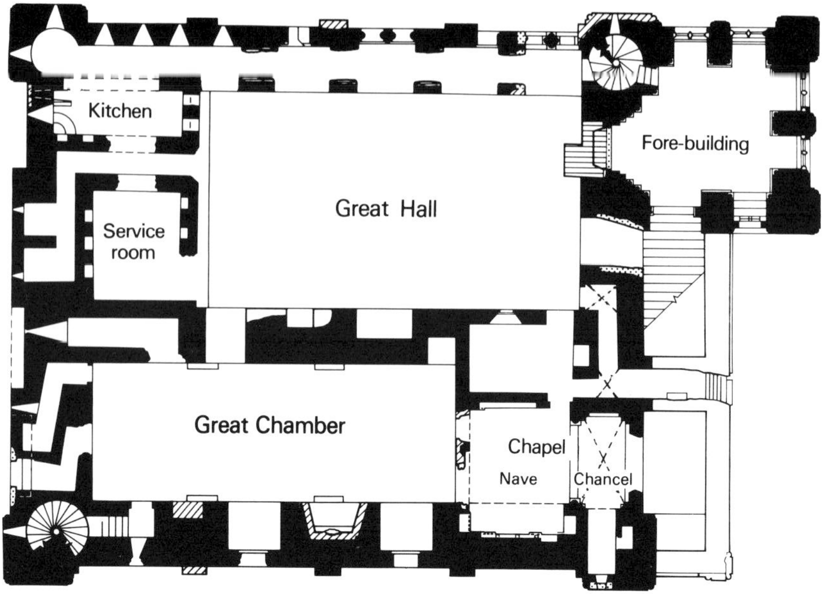

First floor

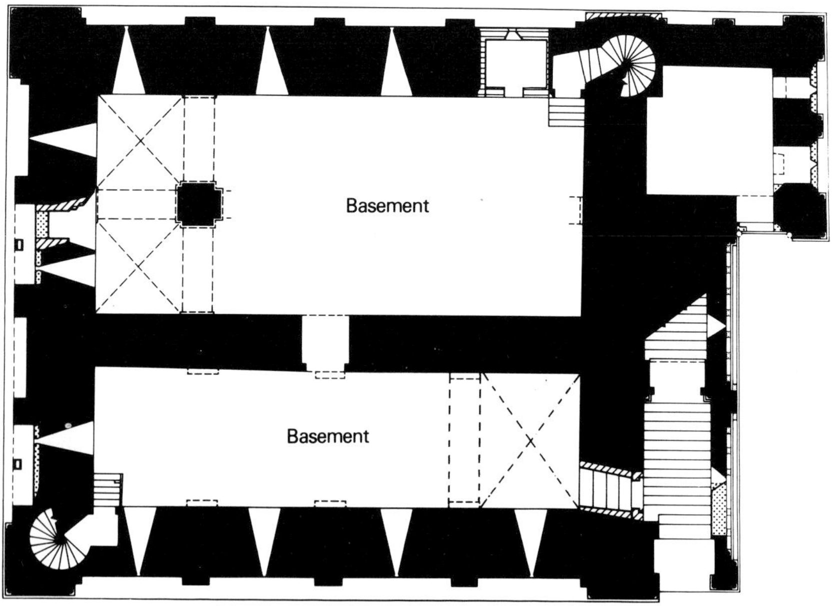

Ground floor

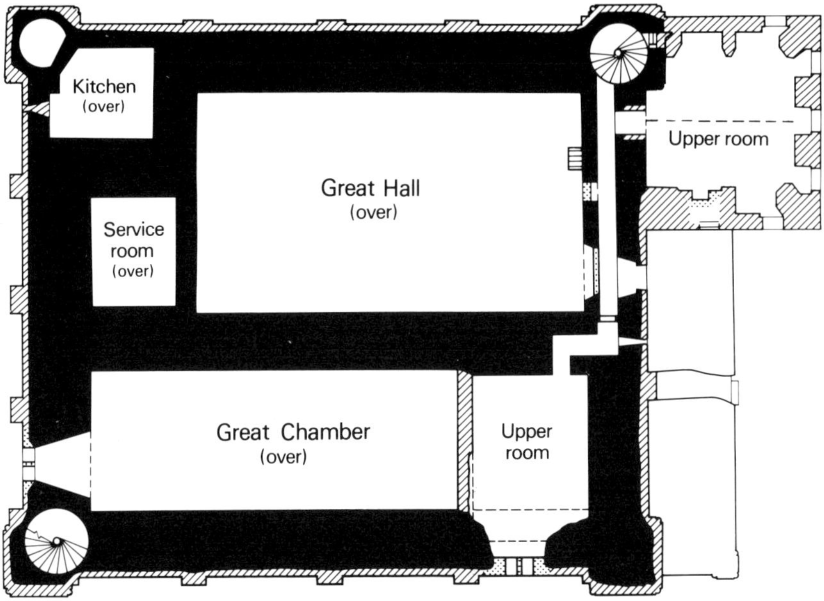

Second floor

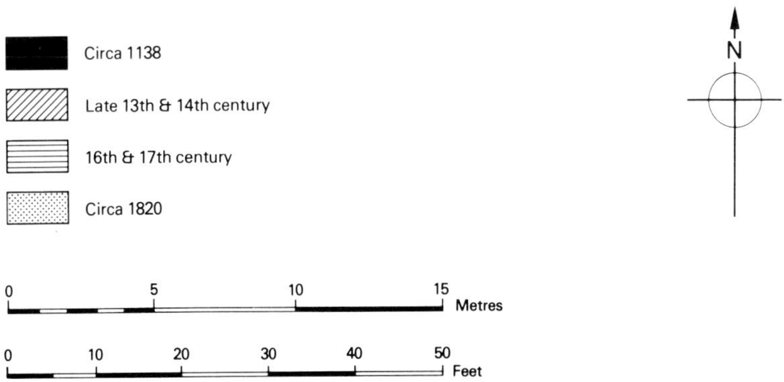

Floor plans of the keep

Plate 8 Keep from the southeast

The keep at Rising measures some 78½ft (24m) east to west by 68½ft (21m) north to south, while to these dimensions the forebuilding, which both provides and defends the entrance on the east side, adds a further 20ft (6m) to the north face and 9ft (2.7m) to the south. The walls of the great tower, which now lacks its crenellated parapet and corner turrets, rise some 50ft (15m) from a battered plinth. The walls of the tower of the forebuilding now rise to the same height from their own battered plinth, and are crowned by an unconvincing looking high-pitched roof which is certainly not original but may date, at least in type, from the time of the late-medieval vault inserted in its upper storey (page 46). The material of the keep is coursed rubble with facings of oolite ashlar, mainly Barnack. The rubble, which contains local, brown carstone, now appears as rather pleasing panels between the buttresses, all of which are faced with ashlar, but there are also large sections of dressed stone on the west front, and still more on the forebuilding. Each of the long north and south sides of the keep has three shallow and plain pilaster buttresses—there is another on the east side behind the forebuilding stairway (Plate 8)—each of which evidently had two string-courses originally, though some are now wanting. These pilasters, it seems, died into the parapet above the line of a string-course which only survives on the south and east sides.

The four corners of the keep itself—that is, excluding the forebuilding which has angle and pilaster buttresses of its own—have clasping or angle buttresses which once rose above the roof line to form four corner turrets. Each is

Plate 9 Keep from the southwest

decorated by three nook shafts, one at each extremity, which evidently rose from moulded bases to cushion capitals at the top immediately beneath the topmost string-course which went all round the keep, but the top of the keep has been so altered in later reparations that a detailed discussion of the present appearance of the upper levels of these angle buttresses is best left until those later works themselves are dealt with (page 40). The details of the window openings—generally speaking, mere loops at ground-floor or basement level, and anything more spacious for obvious reasons confined to the upper stage—are also best left to be described with the description of the rooms they lit, but it may at once be noted that the two-light window high up at the right or east end of the south front is an eighteenth- or nineteenth-century insertion, as is the other two-light window of Early English appearance on the west face.

The west face of the keep has arcading, reminiscent of Norwich, functional in intention, though now much altered from its original arrangement. The left-hand pair of arches come closest to that original arrangement, though the pilaster or respond between them is partly broken away and a later doorway, now blocked, has at some time been inserted on the left side. Each of these two arches masks the vent of a garderobe above it—that is, the pair of garderobes serving the hall at first-floor level inside the keep. Beneath the arches the plinth is brought up higher, and although recent excavation has demonstrated that at first there was no cesspit for the spoil, one was provided later. To the right of this pair of arches there was obviously originally another pair exactly similar and with the same function, this time serving the pair of garderobes opening off the great chamber at first-floor level within. Here, however, the pilaster or respond is entirely broken away, though still visible, and the single recess thus formed arched over with a single and later arch, spoiling the original symmetry. The large window opening immediately above this arch is also incorrect and later, taking the place of one of the four small slits which originally lit and aired the four garderobes, one to each. Between what were the two pairs of arches for the garderobes there is now one very tall arch going almost up to parapet level. Whether this recess was originally arched over, as it is now, is perhaps an open question (the one remaining recess to the left, between the left-hand garderobe and the northwest angle buttress of the keep, it may be noted, is not so arched), though it is very effective in giving the appearance of bold blind arcading to this whole west face of the keep (Plate 9).

The east end of the keep is masked by the forebuilding, which also extends eastward the southern and northern faces. This forebuilding can claim to be among the finest in all England and is the most notable feature of the whole castle, notable especially for its elaborate decoration, unusual in the plain but impressive functionalism of medieval military architecture, though again reminiscent of Norwich and its forebuilding (the former Bigod's Tower), largely destroyed in the nineteenth century. A forebuilding is a normal feature of the twelfth-century keep, its purpose being to cover and defend the principal entrance, usually placed above ground level for obvious security reasons. That at Castle Rising consisted of a straight and covered staircase of two flights leading up to the east face of the keep to the first (and original) floor of the forebuilding tower, through which one passed at right-angles, via an entrance vestibule, into the first main residential floor of the great tower itself. All of its buttresses, both angle and pilaster, are or were decorated with nook shafts with moulded bases and cushion capitals, the buttresses then dying into the wall face with a string-course above. The first and main series of windows in the tower—that is, those of the entrance vestibule—are similarly decorated, and there is more sumptuous decoration on both faces of the staircase building (Plate 10).

On the south front, immediately above the entrance portal, with its round moulded arch there is, first, a corbelled frieze of quatrefoils within diamonds. Above this there is blank arcading of two roll-moulded arches springing from moulded capitals and columns with an axe-work pattern in between them, and with a chevron and a billeted band or string-course respectively above and below. Between the two arches of the arcade there is a carved head which may have been inserted later. Finally, above the chevron band which surmounts the blind arcading, there are two moulded roundels each with a weathered carved head in the centre, apparently one human and one animal, probably later insertions (Plate 8).

Round the corner, on the east face of the staircase building, the same pattern

Plate 10 East face of the keep seen from the gatehouse

(though with variants) of blind arcading with chevron and billet respectively above and below, the whole surmounted by roundels, is, or obviously was, continued. The first arcade had six of the same moulded arches springing from the same moulded capitals and columns again with an axe-work pattern in between, and above its chevron course there remain, though only in part, two of the moulded roundels, each with a central carved head which again is probably a later insertion. The second arcade, with now no trace of axe-work pattern in the background, is taller to correspond with the higher roof line of the second flight of stairs within, and here the arches intersect, three one way and two and two halves the other.

Between the two arcades, and set in the plain pilaster buttress which separates them, there can be seen a ruined postern, in this case an elevated doorway with steps down to it at the end of the narrow passage which traverses at right angles the middle of the staircase within (page 45). Though the passage is original and part of the defences of the stairway, it is very likely that the postern is a late insertion, probably dating from the 'squatter' period when the keep was partly ruined, and in any case could only have been used with the aid of a ladder or some other makeshift and presumably wooden steps.

The forebuilding tower, beyond the staircase building, in addition to its decorated buttresses and grand windows at first-floor level, has or had, on the line of the string-course above those windows, three carved heads on each face. These, like all the other heads on the forebuilding, were probably inserted later, possibly during the fourteenth-century work when the forebuilding tower was heightened (page 46). This tower also has on its south face a tall arched recess or single arcade beneath the southern window, again with shafts and cushion capitals. At the foot of this, leading into the basement of the tower beneath the entrance vestibule, there is a square-headed doorway which is certainly a later insertion in its present form, but may be the replacement of an early or original doorway in the same position. There was no other access to this basement which could only otherwise have been reached by the inconvenient method of a trap-door in the vestibule floor. It is clear from structural evidence that the great windows of the entrance vestibule at first-floor level were originally open (i.e. not glazed) and that their present mullions and transoms are later insertions. It is also clear from external and internal (page 55) evidence that the forebuilding tower has been heightened, most probably in the early fourteenth century, and that its upper storey, above the string-course and the buttresses, is an addition of that time.

It is always advisable, in order to appreciate the whole, to look at the outside of a building before entering it. In the case of the keep at Castle Rising a close inspection will reveal, in addition to the prominent features so far described, some of the evidence which, combined with other evidence inside (and yet other evidence which came to light during the work of conservation by the Department of the Environment), points to the extensive reparation and rebuilding especially of the upper levels of the fabric, again at a date most probably in the early fourteenth century. For example, on the south face of the keep some 12ft (3.7m) below the top there is a more or less horizontal pebbly line of small flints, which rough line can be traced elsewhere round the keep but here is clearest. While there are other indications of changes of masonry at other levels of the great tower, marking pauses and breaks in its construction (which may be no more than seasonal as medieval building was usually abandoned in the winter), this one seems particularly significant as there are changes of style and outright oddities above it. On the south front, for example, and in the south face of the southwest angle buttress, there is, above this line, a pointed lancet different from and later in style than all the other external loops in the building. Again if one moves round to the west face of the keep, there is to be seen, at first-floor level and to the left of the double arcade of the northern pair of garderobe vents, a small window or loop which is not only blocked but has also lost its round head in some later rebuilding.

The tops of the angle buttresses all round the keep, where they formerly rose into the angle turrets now lost, also repay attention. Two are downright peculiar and, most significantly, all of them differ from one another, which is almost inconceivable as the result of original intention or execution. Thus the southwest angle, containing in its southern face the later lancet already noted, has also, to the right of the same south face at the summit, two most peculiar and awkwardly placed corbels not found anywhere else on the keep, and though its nook shafts terminate in cushion capitals, which may represent the original twelfth-century arrangement, there is no string-course above them. The existing treatment of the northwest angle buttress (beside which, to the right, is the headless and blocked window noted above) is even odder. Here the nook shafts have no capitals at all but end with a slight moulding which is the mere continuation of the string-course that is present on this angle. But at the actual angle itself, and above the string-course, there is a cushion capital thus detached from the nook shaft below it—a clear case, it would seem, of a mason re-using twelfth-century stone in some later rebuilding, and not knowing quite what to do with it.

To move on to the northeast angle—that is, next to the forebuilding tower—here the buttress, like those of the forebuilding but alone of those of the keep, dies into the parapet above the string-course (here present again), though the nook shafts have no cushion capitals but only simple mouldings at their summits. Yet now showing in the upper room of the forebuilding (page 56) there is a twelfth-century cushion capital evidently pertaining to this angle of the keep, and it is also evident that the whole right-hand section of this buttress has been rebuilt from the bottom up, to fit the moulded base of the right-hand nook shaft and to encroach upon the fine twelfth-century two-light window adjacent at first-floor level. Finally, the treatment of the top of the southeast angle buttress, next to the forebuilding entrance, differs yet again, with the nook shafts terminating not in cushion capitals but in two simple mouldings or rings (like a cotton reel) above which is the string-course.

The upper level of the keep therefore has evidently had substantial work done upon it at some date after its first building, and the fact that this is not immediately apparent with a deliberate change of style, and involved the re-use of twelfth-century ashlar—for example, the cushion capital at the northwest angle, but also less obviously elsewhere—suggests that the work was not a conscious alteration or modernisation (or even the completion of a building formerly left unfinished) but a reparation and making good of what was ruined or decayed. The decay of a neglected building, of course, is likely to start at the top and spread downwards.

Other evidence, some of which came to light in the course of recent conservation work and not all of which can be seen by visitors, points in the same direction, and shows also that the keep was slightly heightened and its roof-line raised as the result of these reparations. Thus the central spine or cross-wall has been rebuilt and made good in its upper levels, and contained evidence of a former roof earlier and lower than that which can now be traced. The south wall-head of the keep had similarly been rebuilt and contained beneath its summit the top of the twelfth-century chimney pipe of the great chamber below. The north wall-head had likewise been rebuilt with a re-use of twelfth-century ashlar and with quadrant corbels characteristic of the early fourteenth century. The earlier fourteenth century is also the most likely date of the figure-head corbels still in part remaining on both sides of the great hall (but now gone from the great chamber, page 53) as evident insertions for a new roof at that time, and also of the doorway which now connects the great chamber and the chapel (page 53). The early fourteenth century is again the very likely date of the insertion of the vault in the entrance vestibule of the forebuilding tower (page 46), and therefore of the heightening of that tower to incorporate a new upper storey (page 56).

While there is no absolute certainty that all these alterations, amendments and curiosities, noted in the last few paragraphs, are of the same date and the result of one major operation, it may seem significant that they are almost all in the upper levels of the building, and the structural evidence does seem to match the possible historical pattern of the lordship of Rising previously discussed (page 17), and both to suggest a period of neglect and consequent decay in the early Montalt period, and a subsequent large-scale reparation and restoration most probably by Robert de Montalt, the last of his line, before 1329 when he died.

Forebuilding

One enters the keep through the main entrance, described above, into the forebuilding on the south front. The view straight up the two flights of the entrance staircase, through the middle doorway to the doorway of the vestibule

Plate 11 Forebuilding as it might have been, from a reconstruction drawing by Alan Sorrell

Plate 12 Forebuilding stairway

above, is the grandest and most evocative in the whole castle (Plate 11). The staircase was formerly covered with a low-pitched roof leaning into the main wall of the keep on the left, some traces of which can still be seen. There was no portcullis at the entrance, but there are drawbar holes to bar the door. Over the groined entrance passage in the thickness of the wall (6ft; 1.8m) as one enters there is a deep recess, presumably to reduce the weight upon the vault. On the right as one begins to mount the first flight of steps there is a splayed loop high up, and immediately on the left a brick doorway leading down some steps into the basement of the keep. This entrance to the basement is certainly of late medieval date and there is no trace of any earlier predecessor.

Fifteen steps 8ft (2.4m) wide lead up to the middle doorway with a landing 5ft (1.5m) deep behind it. The doorway has again a roll-moulded arch and flanking columns with cushion capitals, and is made yet more handsome by the decorated jambs of the door which stand forward like columns and formerly supported an inner order of the arch above. Again there is no portcullis, though there are drawbar holes, but above and just in front of the door, directly above visitors' heads, there is a *meurtrière* or murder-hole for its better defence (though not with boiling oil), worked from a mural passage in the transverse wall which divides the entrance staircase into two and through which this doorway passes. During recent conservation work a pit beneath the staircase was discovered at this stage, though it was lined with later brick.

Beyond the landing the second flight of nineteen steps, still 8ft (2.4m) wide, ascends to the doorway at the top, into the entrance vestibule, much like the middle doorway below it, with roll-moulded head, flanking columns with cushion capitals (but no protruding jambs) and with drawbar holes. On the way up there is a splayed loop on the right, and on the left a very crude and awkwardly placed forced entrance or later doorway into the first floor of the keep, most certainly not original but hacked out (possibly in place of a former loop) when the proper entrance from the vestibule was blocked.

Entrance vestibule

The entrance vestibule, through which access was gained to the state apartments of the lords of Rising on the first floor of the keep, is still very grand in spite of later alteration and mutilation later still. Its dominant feature, appropriately, is the splendid (though slightly botched) portal on the left into the great hall (Plate 12), with its lofty arch of three orders worked in chevron and other ornaments, roll-mouldings in between, a triple group of columns on either side with cushion capitals, the plinths set unusually high off the ground (perhaps for steps up). Some time in the philistine Tudor age this splendid entrance (again reminiscent of Norwich) was blocked and a fireplace inserted, presumably in the 'squatter' period of the keep's history, when the principal apartments had become uninhabitable, and the glory had departed. The medieval tiles now displayed (behind glass) above the fireplace have nothing to do with the castle and chiefly confuse; they were discovered in the 1840s at a deserted tile kiln in neighbouring Bawsey, and set up here by the Honourable Mary Howard.

The windows of the vestibule, two north, two east, and one south, round-headed, deeply recessed, groined, with flanking columns with cushion capitals, are basically original and were originally open (unglazed) as at Norwich, to form an arcade. As such, however, they evidently had shutters for which a pair of drawbar holes can be seen high up on each of them except the southern. The stone mullions and transoms are later insertions of the fifteenth or sixteenth centuries, and the southern window has a quite modern timber casement.

There was a string-course, now hacked away, about the room at the level of the present upper transoms. The vault, ill-executed and spoiling the original Romanesque proportions of the room, is an evident insertion, put in when this vestibule tower of the forebuilding was heightened by the addition of its present upper storey and chamber. It springs from five corbels (one of which is contrived from a twelfth-century window shaft) of two distinct patterns, one foliated and the other mutilated beyond recognition. It is the former, with its naturalistic foliage and mouldings above and below, which can scarcely be later than the 1320s and which, though it could be earlier, allows one to suppose an early fourteenth-century date for the whole work, which is thus most likely to have been undertaken by Robert de Montalt, lord of Rising from 1299 to 1329 (page 17). The the right of the grand but blocked main portal there is a small original doorway leading to the northeast newel staircase or vice of the keep, and above it to the right there is a small blocked lancet reminiscent of that on the southwest face of the keep (page 41).

Access to the keep proper or great tower itself can now be gained either by this small doorway from the vestibule or through the later and forced doorway at the bottom of the main entrance stairway in the forebuilding. Internally it is divided horizontally into two storeys, a basement and a first and residential floor containing all the principal apartments, though there is also an upper level at the east end comprising a chamber above the chapel, which is original, as well as the chamber above the vestibule in the forebuilding, which is a fourteenth-century addition. Communication between the floors, and from basement to roof, parapets and turrets, was provided by two newels or vices, one in the northeast and one in the southwest angle, the latter at present closed to visitors.

As with most great towers of the period, to give greater structural strength as well as more internal partition, there is also a vertical division, north and south, by a cross-wall running east to west, dividing the interior of the keep into two unequal parts, the northern the larger. Because the roof is gone, and the floors of the great hall and great chamber, with all decoration and rich furnishings, an effort of the imagination must be made to realise that this was no stark fortress or barracks, but a nobleman's fortified residence, lived in and lived in nobly. A

Plate 13 Blocked Norman doorway to the great hall

kind of timber gallery has been erected at the east end, so that the whole interior can be seen and its various parts easily reached.

Basement

Plate 14 Window jamb in great hall lobby

The basement of the keep is at ground level and must be supposed to have been used principally for storage. Its northern division measures some 58 by 25ft (18 by 8m) and is vaulted at the west end (with the kitchen above), one surviving pillar bearing both longitudinal and transverse arches. Two other central pillars, however, formerly stood in line (the base of one of them, a simple rectangle, recently rediscovered) bearing longitudinal arches only, to support the joists of the vanished timber ceiling of the rest of this division. The springing of these arches east and west can still be seen and the well was situated between the two vanished piers. The room was aired and lit by round-headed loops, high up in deeply splayed recesses, four in the north wall and two in the west.

The most easterly recess in the north wall, next to the northeast vice, has at some time been converted into a curious mezzanine and mural chamber, inaccessible now except by ladder from the basement floor, but perhaps once gained from the vice, which ends in a small groined landing more or less at the appropriate level, before leading on to four further steps down into the basement. At the west end of this northern division, in the vaulted section, a later doorway was at some time forced out through the west wall of the keep, between the two loops, but is now blocked again. A round-headed and groined doorway 4ft (1.2m) wide off-centre in the cross-wall leads into the southern basement: it has drawbar holes to the north, on which side later brickwork spoils its appearance.

The southern basement measures about 58 by 16ft (18 by 5m). The room being narrower than its northern counterpart, there are no central piers but three pairs of corbels facing north and south, which do not all match, and which must have been intended to provide the springing for the transverse arches of a vault. In the event, however, only the eastern bay (with the chapel above it) was so vaulted, the other two pairs of corbels evidently being left with no function, as there are beam holes above them for the joists of a timber ceiling. This basement was aired and lit by four recesses and splayed loops, like those in the northern basement, in its south wall, but needed only one in the west wall. In the southwest corner there is the newel staircase, ending like its northeastern counterpart in a small landing or lobby above floor level, with steps down. At the east end, in the vaulted section, there is the later, forced and brick-lined opening, with steps up, to the late medieval doorway giving on to the foot of the entrance stairway in the forebuilding.

The first floor of the keep contained the state apartments and the principal residential accommodation of the lord of Rising. Like the basement below, it is divided into two unequal parts by the cross-wall. North of the cross-wall, the largest apartment is thought to have been the great hall, with the kitchens and domestic offices opening off it at the west end; south of the crosswall, the large apartment is thought to have been the great chamber, with the chapel and ante-chapel situated east of it. Each of the two main apartments is served by two garderobes set in the thickness of the west wall.

Great hall

The great hall measures some 47 by 23ft (14 by 7m). It has lost both its floor and its roof and therefore most of its grandeur. Its principal entrance was at its east end—that is the grand entrance to the keep itself from the vestibule in the forebuilding, now blocked and further disfigured by the brick chimney-stack of the Tudor fireplace inserted in it. Since the late forced doorway from the top of the forebuilding stairs (Plate 11), crudely replacing the blocked grand entrance (Plate 12), no longer gives access to the hall, it is now entered via an original small doorway from the northwest newel staircase. This leads not into the hall itself but into a small groined entrance lobby in the thickness of the north wall and formed out of the first window opening. The lobby is distinguished by what is now one of the most splendid individual features of the keep, namely the richly worked two-light window, the scalloped capitals and moulded bases, but remarkable especially for the cable and interlaced carving of its central shaft (Plate 14). The left window was, unfortunately, crudely repaired in brick.

It is best to note at once that—from this point onwards to the lobby in the same north wall at the west end of the hall, and thus traversing the second, third and fourth window embrasures—the present mural gallery is a later insertion, hacked through, no doubt, in the 'squatter' period when the floors had gone and when, as now, there was no other easy means of getting from the small habitable rooms at the east end of the keep to those at the west end. The three window embrasures through which the mural gallery now passes were, therefore, originally embrasures and nothing more, serving the deeply recessed windows which lit the hall from the north. The three windows themselves as they now appear are, to the left and right, tri-lobed, but of unequal opening, while the central one is of two lights and square headed. This therefore, though now much worn and weathered, was originally marked out by distinct and grander treatment, and it is to be noted that it is opposite to, and axially aligned with, the recess in the south wall of the hall (see below) which almost certainly marked out the lord of Rising's place at table. The mural gallery now ends in an original small groined lobby in the thickness of the wall at the west end of the hall, through which one reached the kitchen. As this was thus used by mere servitors passing from the splendours of the hall to the service quarters, it is lit by a mere loop, and the opening from the hall (a doorway rather than a window embrasure) is markedly smaller than the others (Plate 14). At this end of the hall, however, the pier between this opening and the next is decorated with roll moulding at its angles, which may mark a screens passage here dividing off the kitchen, buttery, pantry and garderobes (yet to be described).

The hall was thus lit chiefly by windows in the north wall, and could be entered and left on the same side. The opposite south wall (the cross-wall of the keep) has, more or less centrally, a large round-headed recess, 8ft (2.4m) wide and 5ft (1.5m) deep. It looks like a fireplace but has no flue, and its probable purpose was to give architectural emphasis to the lord's place at his table, which presumably ran lengthwise, east to west. There are similar features in the two halls at Pickering Castle and in the hall of the Great Tower at Chepstow. To the right, or west, of this there is another smaller rounded-headed recess, now 5ft (1.5m) above floor level, which may be a cupboard and just might represent a former and original doorway between the hall and the chamber south of it, since the present doorway—to the right again and in the southwest corner of the hall, now inaccessible—does not look entirely convincing. At the other, east, end of this south wall of the hall there is a doorway with segmental head leading into the ante-chapel, and above and to the right of it a window lighting the same.

The east wall of the hall can be seen from the mural gallery or from the various openings at the western end. It is marred by the blocked grand entrance and the chimney stack. Near the top of it one can see the gentle slope of a former roof-line, which is not the original but slightly higher, and goes with the fourteenth-century figurehead corbels formerly ranged along the north and south walls of both hall (where some survive) and great chamber (where all are wanting). Beneath this roof-line, at the level of the corbels from which timbers supporting the roof once sprang, there is a horizontal band or string-course of bold chevron pattern. There are also, high up in the wall, two window openings. The first and smaller, immediately right of the chimney-stack, is rounded-headed and original, partly blocked, and sits on the chevron band. It brought light into the upper level of the hall via a mural passage which exists in the east wall of the keep at this level (page 56). To the right of it there is a much bigger round-headed window opening with the same function but now entirely blocked. Because this opening now comes down so far as to break through the chevron band, it is presumably a later insertion or alteration, but it may well replace an original feature not very much smaller since it corresponds to a large and original window opening opposite to it, looking out, on the other side of

Plate 15 West end of great hall above its basement

the mural passage behind it (page 57). Beneath the chevron band, at floor level, there is, to the right of the blocked main entrance and chimney stack, the later forced opening and, right of this again, a small, original and segmental-headed doorway which leads, by way of a mural passage ending in a T-junction, both to the *meurtrière* (and later postern) above the forebuilding staircase (pages 40, 45) and to the ante-chapel.

In the west end of the hall, in addition to the access to the kitchen via the lobby in the north wall, there were two openings only. A little to the right of centre a tall, narrow, round-headed doorway leads—and originally led only—to the two garderobes, each with a loop, serving the hall in the west wall of the keep. The passage leading to the garderobes is now broken through both right and left, respectively into the kitchen and service room (buttery? pantry?) south of it. Originally the southern service room was entered only by a doorway, still there but now much mutilated, on the south or left side of the west wall of the hall. The room itself (which stands on the vaulted section of the basement below it) is rectangular, measuring some 12 by 8ft (3.7 by 2.4m), and its principal features are the recesses or cupboards in its west (3) and east (2) walls, and the curious low arches of relief in its north and south walls, in the former case broken through into the garderobe passage. There was evidently a timber roof for which one corbel and some joist holes are still extant. These in turn have sometimes led to the notion that there was an upper room in the vacant space above, but this is impossible as any room in that position would have had no access and no light.

Kitchen

The kitchen on the other side of the garderobe passage situated in the northwest corner of the keep, vaulted above as it is also vaulted below, is perhaps the most interesting surviving feature of Castle Rising, as the cooking arrangements in castle keeps are by no means always so obvious, even to the point of being in many cases something of a mystery. There is an almost exact analogy, in the same position, in the keep at Norwich. In the northwest corner, constructed in the northwest angle of the keep, there is a great circular hearth and fireplace, clearly for cooking, with two tiers of loops or vents for smoke and steam, the whole cavity gathered in above to form a circular chimney shaft. To the left of the fireplace, in the west wall, there is a floor-level drain for sluicing out, with a loop left and above it, and left of this again, in the southwest corner of the room, there are the remains of an oven. In the south wall and in the east wall (where they have been broken through into the hall) there are recesses or cupboards like those in the service room described in the previous paragraph; in the south wall there was also a low relieving arch which, like its opposite number in the north wall of the service room, has been broken through to give direct but crude access to one room from the other across the garderobe passage. Further light and ventilation were brought into the lofty kitchen by a series of loops, three below and two above, in its north wall which is also the north wall of the keep.

Great chamber

The great chamber, occupying most of the southern half of the keep at first-floor level, was formerly entered from the great hall by a doorway through the cross-wall which separates the two apartments, but, like the hall, having lost both its floor and its roof, can now be seen (and imagined) only from the basement below it or from the chapel to the east of it. It was lit by two windows in the south wall, both deeply recessed in round-headed embrasures, the left window (not the other, which is plain) being tri-lobed and thus probably both retaining the original pattern and matching the similar tri-lobed windows in the hall. Between the two windows is a massive fireplace, now brick-lined but an original feature since the twelfth-century ashlar chimney-pipe was revealed in recent conservation work on the wallhead above it. Also in the south wall, to the right of the right-hand window, there is a large, tall, round-headed recess of uncertain purpose, now blocked below the level of its arch. To the right of this again there is a segmental doorway with steps up, leading, via a small lobby and passage with a loop, to the southwest vice or newel staircase which communicated with all levels of the keep but is at present closed to visitors.

At the west end of the great chamber in the west wall of the keep, high up and to the left, there is the pointed two-light window in a large round-headed recess, the whole now identified not as Early English but as an eighteenth- or nineteenth-century insertion. This being therefore unacceptable as a medieval feature, there is no authentic evidence for any accommodation above first-floor level at this end of the keep. Also in the west wall of the great chamber, at floor level, there are two tall, narrow, round-headed doorways, each leading via a skewed passage to a garderobe in the thickness of the wall. The right-hand doorway has a rebate for a door; inside, at the turning of the passage and just visible to visitors, there is the interesting and uncommon feature of a urinal. (There is another, though of different design, in the later twelfth-century keep at Orford in Suffolk.) As these two garderobes off the great chamber at Castle Rising have separate doorways and only one has a urinal, it may not be too fanciful to suggest that the one on the left was for ladies and the other for gentlemen. Each garderobe was originally aired and lit by a loop, though in the left-hand one this has been replaced, probably in recent times, by an improbable and inconveniently large window opening.

Along the north wall of the chamber from west (left) to east there is, first, a narrow round-headed doorway which upon investigation leads into a long narrow closet running east to west in the thickness of the cross-wall, ending with a loop in the west wall of the keep; next, the larger doorway leading from and to the hall; and last, at the east end of the chamber, a large round-headed recess, presumably a cupboard. The great chamber, like the hall, evidently received handsome figurehead corbels, now wanting, along north and south walls in the fourteenth century when the keep was reroofed.

Chapel

The wall at the east end of the great chamber divides it from the chapel. Originally there was no intercommunication at the point, access to the chapel being from the hall, but the existing fine and pointed doorway was later inserted, probably in the early fourteenth century (the aperture or hole in the wall to the right of it is merely the accident of ruin).

If the kitchen is the most interesting apartment in the keep, the chapel—in the diametrically opposite corner (compare with Norwich again) and standing above the vaulted section of the basement beneath it—is and was meant to be architecturally the most beautiful and ornate. Its architectural treatment, indeed, marks it out for what it is, so that even Harrod, who did not recognise it as a chapel (and in this has had some modern followers) nevertheless described it as 'the handsomest room in the whole building.' It consists of three divisions of which the largest, serving as the nave or main body of the chapel, is an almost square rectangle measuring 13 by 14ft (3.9 by 4.2m) and was vaulted at least from the fourteenth century. It had also a magnificent Norman arcading about it, with detached shafts with cushion capitals and roll-moulded arches, now much damaged and part gone, on the lower half of its north, south and west walls. On the west wall this has been pierced and broken into by the insertion of the fourteenth-century doorway. In the north wall above the former arcading there are two high small windows, mere slits, double splayed and original, which allow the ante-chapel beyond to borrow light from the chapel. Here, too, in the north wall to the right, is the original doorway from the ante-chapel.

In the south wall, above the arcade of four bays, there has been a large and fine window, now much damaged, evidently of five lights (cinquefoil), set, like the arcade itself on this side, in a deep recess arched over and with lateral recesses in the jambs. The east side of the nave is given over to the handsome chancel arch, of 7ft 6in (2.3m) span, moulded and decorated with a lozenge or diamond pattern, with shafts with scalloped capitals in front of the piers. The small chancel beyond, constructed entirely within the thickness of the main east wall of the keep (where it is masked by the forebuilding beyond), is elaborate again, vaulted, groined and ribbed with traces of red-painted chevrons on the ribs, and with a sort of non-boss consisting of four opposed crowned heads at the intersection of the ribs for the suspension of an altar lamp. There are also nook shafts with fluted capitals in its four corners, and an east window, evidently of three lights, with a string-course of chevron below it, looking over the forebuilding. To the right of the chancel and opening off it there is a small plain and vaulted closet, presumably the vestry, running south with a blocked loop in the south wall and a recess or aumbry in the east.

Ante-chapel

The ante-chapel lies between the chapel and the hall and thus north of the former, communicating with it by the doorway in the north wall of the nave, which has a rebate for a door on the ante-chapel side. It is a rather plain, rectangular room 9 by 13ft (2.7 by 3.9m) and is constructed partly on the vault of the basement below and partly in the thickness of the cross-wall, which may account for the rather clumsy arrangement of its own vault. It is lit, not very well, by a deeply recessed window in its north wall which borrows light from the hall beyond (and which, if it is later, must surely have replaced an original), and by the two doubly splayed loops high up in the south wall, borrowing light from the chapel. In the centre of its east wall there is a round-headed recess or aumbry. South of this is the opening to the passage which leads both to the *meurtrière* above the forebuilding staircase and, by turning left, back to the hall, and north of the aumbry, in the north wall, the entrance direct from the hall. It is worth mentioning that, as all three doorways in the ante-chapel are original, there were always two ways into it from the hall, either direct or round by the passageway adjoining which leads also to the *meurtrière,* and in this

Plate 16 Southeast corner of the castle chapel

arrangement may be seen that juxtaposition and combination of residential and military functions which is the fundamental characteristic of a castle.

Upper levels

It is now clear that in the beginning the keep of Castle Rising had no third stage—that is, no accommodation between the principal and state apartments on the first floor, just described, and the wall-heads, parapets and turrets at the top—except for one chamber only, directly above the chapel nave. That chamber was, and still is, somewhat inconveniently reached by a long narrow mural passage in the thickness of the east wall of the keep, running off south from the northeast newel staircase. It seems ill situated to be the private or sleeping chamber of any important person; it may have been, perhaps, a guardroom for those watching on the roof, or it may have been the chaplain's chamber—compare with the separate 'suite' by the chapel for the chaplain at Orford. In any event, the Castle Rising donjon is lacking in those small mural chambers, presumably for sleeping or retiring, found frequently in twelfth-century keeps, especially those of the next generation. These original arrangements were later slightly altered by the provision of one more upper chamber in the forebuilding tower, which evidently received a new upper storey when it was vaulted and heightened, probably in the early fourteenth century.

One gains these upper levels by the northeast vice, ascending off the forebuilding entrance vestibule or the lobby in the northeast corner of the great hall. On the way up there is an original opening on the left giving into a passageway and steps up, which must have formerly led on to the roof and fighting platform of the forebuilding tower before it was heightened but is now blocked by the vault of the vestibule inserted probably in the early fourteenth century. Eight steps above this opening one reaches the original mural passage running off to the south within the east wall of the keep.

While the newel staircase itself continues seventeen more steps to the ramparts, a little way within the passage there is a doorway on the left into the upper chamber of the forebuilding tower. This room is some 16ft (4.8m) square, has some very nice medieval encaustic tiles (which have the appearance of an original feature) in its floor, and a lofty but obviously later and clumsily inserted vault ascending into the curious steep-pitched roof of the forebuilding, of which it is the cause. The window openings were round-headed inside but shoulder-headed outside; they have been partly obscured and partly arched over by the later vault, and are disagreeably fitted with rectangular wooden casements of a still later date. There were seven of them as may be seen from outside, three to the east and two each respectively north and south, but one to the north is now obviously blocked and another to the south is entirely hidden behind the later fireplace and chimney.

Occupying much of the west wall, and containing the doorway, there is a large, arched recess which is the relieving arch of the grand entrance from the vestibule into the keep immediately below it. On the right (north) side of this recess there is a twelfth-century shaft with cushion capital which does not at all belong to the room, and is presumably to be understood in association with the arch and with the keep, of which it was presumably an external ornament above the level of the original forebuilding roof. There is a good deal of evidence to indicate that this upper chamber is an addition, presumably of the early fourteenth century, when the forebuilding tower containing it was heightened, and this out-of-place twelfth-century feature seems further confirmation. By now this still attractive room has for a long time formed, in association with the vestibule below it, the only inhabitable quarter of the castle, which no doubt accounts for the eighteenth- or early nineteenth-century grate in the fireplace.

Outside the upper chamber of the forebuilding the narrow mural passage runs straight from the newel staircase for some 32ft (9.6m). On the right, beyond the doorway to the chamber on the left, there is the smaller and original window opening into the roof-space of the hall; it is partly blocked, presumably for safety reasons, in its lower half. Beyond this is the much larger window opening into the same level of the hall, now entirely blocked. Though it does not look genuine it probably replaces a fairly large original to match the original and generous window opening opposite it, on the left (east) side of the passage, now fitted with a wooden casement. Beyond this there is a rebate for a door, and beyond that, on the left, a loop—at which stage the passage turns through two right angles, right and left, to lead into the room above the chapel nave. Now without a floor, the room is inaccessible, but looking across it one can see the brick back of the bogus, eighteenth- or nineteenth-century two-light window in its south wall which is the south wall of the keep.

From this chamber, like everyone else for the last 800 years and more, visitors must now return along the passage to the newel staircase they ascended. There is at present no access to the top of the walls.

Further reading

For the subject of castle in general

A J TAYLOR, 'Military Architecture' in *Medieval England*, edited by A L Poole, Oxford, 1958.

R ALLEN BROWN, *English Castles*, London, 1976.

For Castle Rising in particular

WILLIAM TAYLOR, *The History and Antiquities of Castle Rising, Norfolk,* Lynn and London, *s.d.*

H HARROD, 'Castle Rising' in *Norfolk Archaeology,* volume iv, 1855.

H L BRADFER-LAWRENCE, *Castle Rising,* 1954.

Glossary

ARCADE	Series of arches on columns or piers
ASHLAR	Squared hewn blocks of stone laid in regular courses with fine vertical joints
AUMBRY	Cupboard or recess in a wall for sacramental vessels
BAILEY	Walled enclosure or courtyard of a castle; ward
BARBICAN	Outward extension of a gateway protecting the entrance from attack
BARREL VAULT	Continuous arched vault of semicircular section; tunnel vault
BASTION	Projection from the outer walls of a castle or fortification from which the garrison can see, and defend by flanking fire, the ground before the ramparts
BATTER	Inclined face of a wall
BATTLEMENTS	Indented parapet covering defenders from enemy observation and fire; crenellation
BILLET	Ornamental moulding used in Norman architecture, consisting of raised cylindrical or rectangular blocks at regular intervals

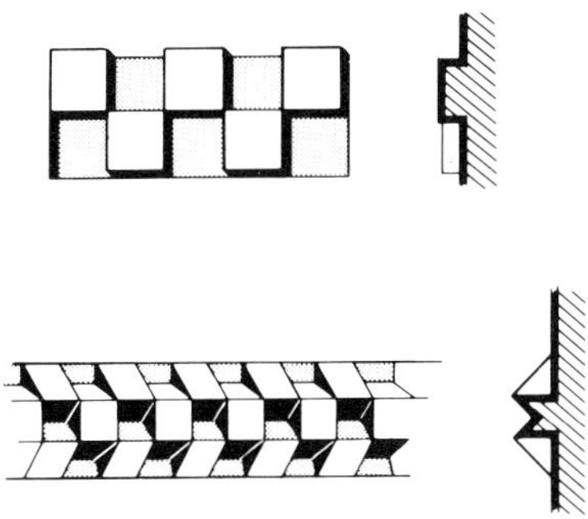

Billet

BULWARK	Defensive wall
BUTTERY	Storeroom where drink (especially ale), butter, cheese, bread and other provisions were kept and issued
BUTTRESS	Masonry built against a wall to give additional strength

CAPITAL	Uppermost part of a column or shaft, often decorated

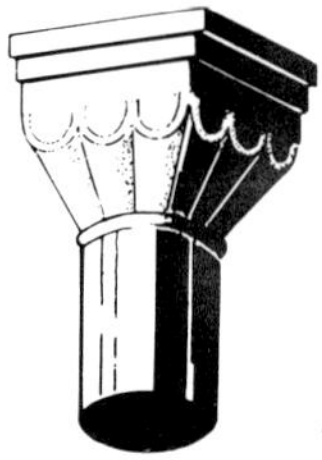

Scalloped capital

CASEMATE	Vaulted room with embrasures, built into the thickness of the ramparts or other fortifications and used as a barracks or battery or both
CHAMFERED	Bevelled symmetrically at edge or corner
CHEVRON	Architectural ornament in the form of an inverted V
CLAUSTRAL	Pertaining to cloister
CLOISTER	Four-sided enclosure between monastic buildings and the church with a covered walk or alley along each side; the centre of monastic life
CORBEL	Stone or wooden projection from a wall to support a weight

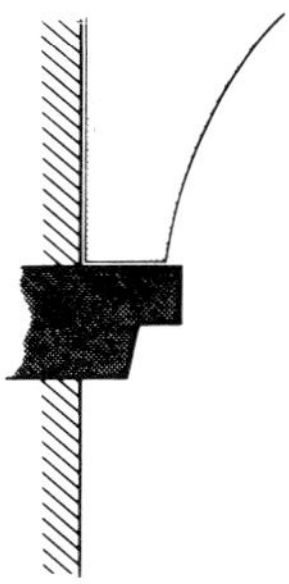

Corbel

CRENELLATION	Battlements

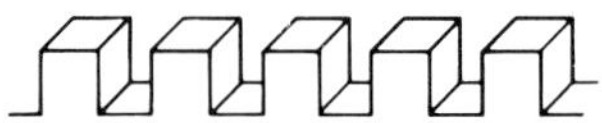

Crenellation (battlements)

CURTAIN WALL	Wall enclosing a castle or one its parts
CUSHION CAPITAL	Cubic capital with lower angles rounded off to fit a circular shaft

DISPENSARY	Place in which medicines were dispensed; room for the relief of the sick poor
DONJON	Keep; great tower
DRAW BAR	Bar to secure a door or gate from the inside
DRAWBRIDGE	Wooden bridge which can be raised towards a gateway by ropes or chains attached to its outer end
EMBRASURE	Splayed opening in a wall for admitting light or shooting through
ENCEINTE	Main line of towers and curtain walls, as distinct from outworks
ENFEOFF	To hand over as a fief
ENGAGED COLUMN	Column attached to or partly sunk into a wall
ESCHEATOR	Officer who certified on escheat when property or a fief reverted to the Crown
FIEF	Land or estate granted (and inherited) by feudal tenure in 'fee' or return for service
FOREBUILDING	Projection containing stairs leading to first floor of keep
GARDEROBE	Latrine, normally discharging into a cesspit or through an outer wall into the moat or onto the berm (the space between the base of the wall and the moat)
GROIN	Edge formed by the intersection of two vaults
HALF SHAFT	Half a column (halved vertically) attached to a wall
IN TAIL	To settle land, an estate etc, on a number of persons in succession so that it cannot be dealt with by any one possessor as an absolute owner
KEEP	Great tower; donjon
LANCET	High and narrow window with a pointed head

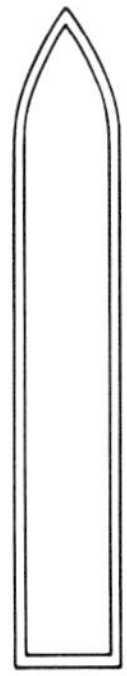

Lancet

LOOP	Narrow opening to discharge arrows through or to admit light; *cross loop,* loop in the form of a cross

MERLON	Section of parapet wall between the open section of battlement, sometimes pierced with slits
MEURTRIÈRE	Hole pierced in vaulted top of gate or passageway for attacking the enemy when trying to force entry
MOTTE	An artificial mound of earth forming the stronghold of an eleventh- or twelfth-century castle
MURAL GALLERY	Gallery constructed within the thickness of a wall
NAVE	Part of a church extending westwards from the screen or crossing, separated from the side aisles by pillars
NEWEL STAIRS	Circular stair with tapered steps which wind around a central pillar or newel; vice
ORDER	System of base, column, capital and entablature, based on antique Greek or Roman models. There are four principal models whose details tend to follow a fixed pattern: Doric, Ionic, Composite, Corinthian
PALISADE	Palings of strong timber
PARAPET	Screen or rampart covering troops from enemy observation and fire
PILASTER	Square column attached to a wall
PLINTH	Projecting masonry, often with decorative mouldings, at the base of a wall
PIPE ROLL	Annual roll of accounts rendered to the Exchequer by sheriffs and other royal bailiffs
PORTCULLIS	Iron-shod wooden grille suspended by chains in grooves in front of a gate and let down to ground level for additional security
POSTERN	Back or secondary door or gate
QUATREFOIL	Four-lobed tracery
QUOINS	Dressed stones used to finish external corners of buildings

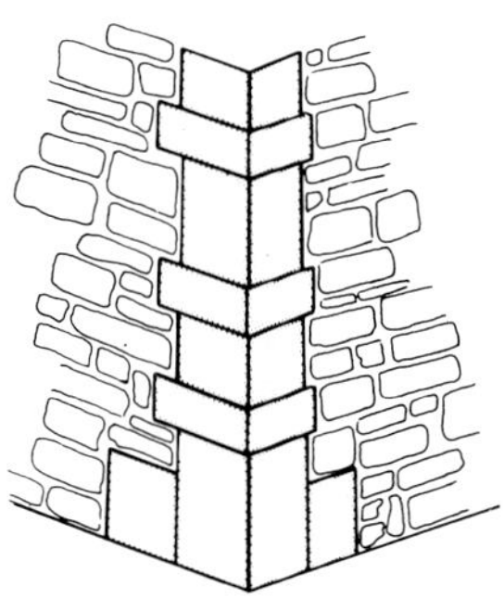

Quoin stones

RAMPART	Wall or bank of excavated earth surrounding a castle from which the defenders repelled attack
REBATE	Recess in a door jamb into which the door fits
RELIEVING ARCH	Plain arch built into a wall above a true arch or lintel to relieve it of some of the load and thrust
RERE-WALL	A protective parapet at the rear of curtain wall
REVETMENT	Retaining wall built to support or hold back a mass of earth or water
SCALLOP	Shape in a series of curves or scallops
SCREEN	Wooden partition at the lower or kitchen end of a hall
SEISIN	Possession of land by freehold
SERVITOR	Male personal or domestic attendant
SHAFT	Part of a column between the base and the capital; often one of a group of two or more clustered columns of lesser diameter; small or subordinate pillar
SPANDREL	Space between the shoulder of an arch and the surrounding moulding
SPRINGER	Lowest stone of an arch or vaulting rib
STRING COURSE	Moulding or projecting band running horizontally across the façade of a building or around its walls
TOLBOOTH	Customs, tolls
TRACERY	Decorative work formed by the branching of verticals (mullions) in the upper part of a window
UNDERCROFT	Vaulted room or cellar, usually at or just below ground level
VAULT	Arched ceiling or roof of stone or brick

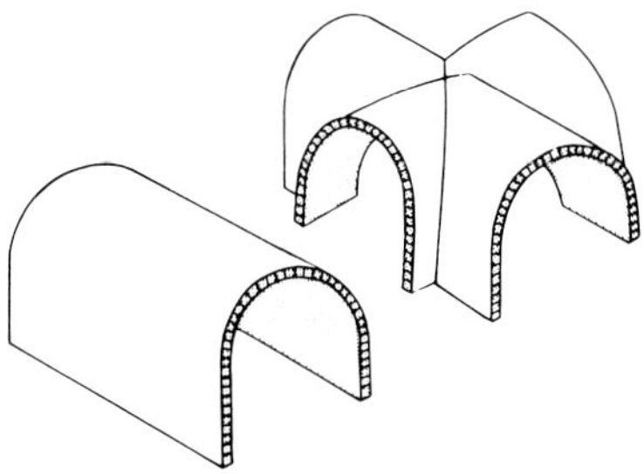

Tunnel and groined vault

VICE	Circular stairway; newel stairs; spiral staircase winding around a central pillar or newel post
WAINSCOT	Wood (normally oak) panelling on lower part of wall of a room